# FINE DETAILS MANDALA

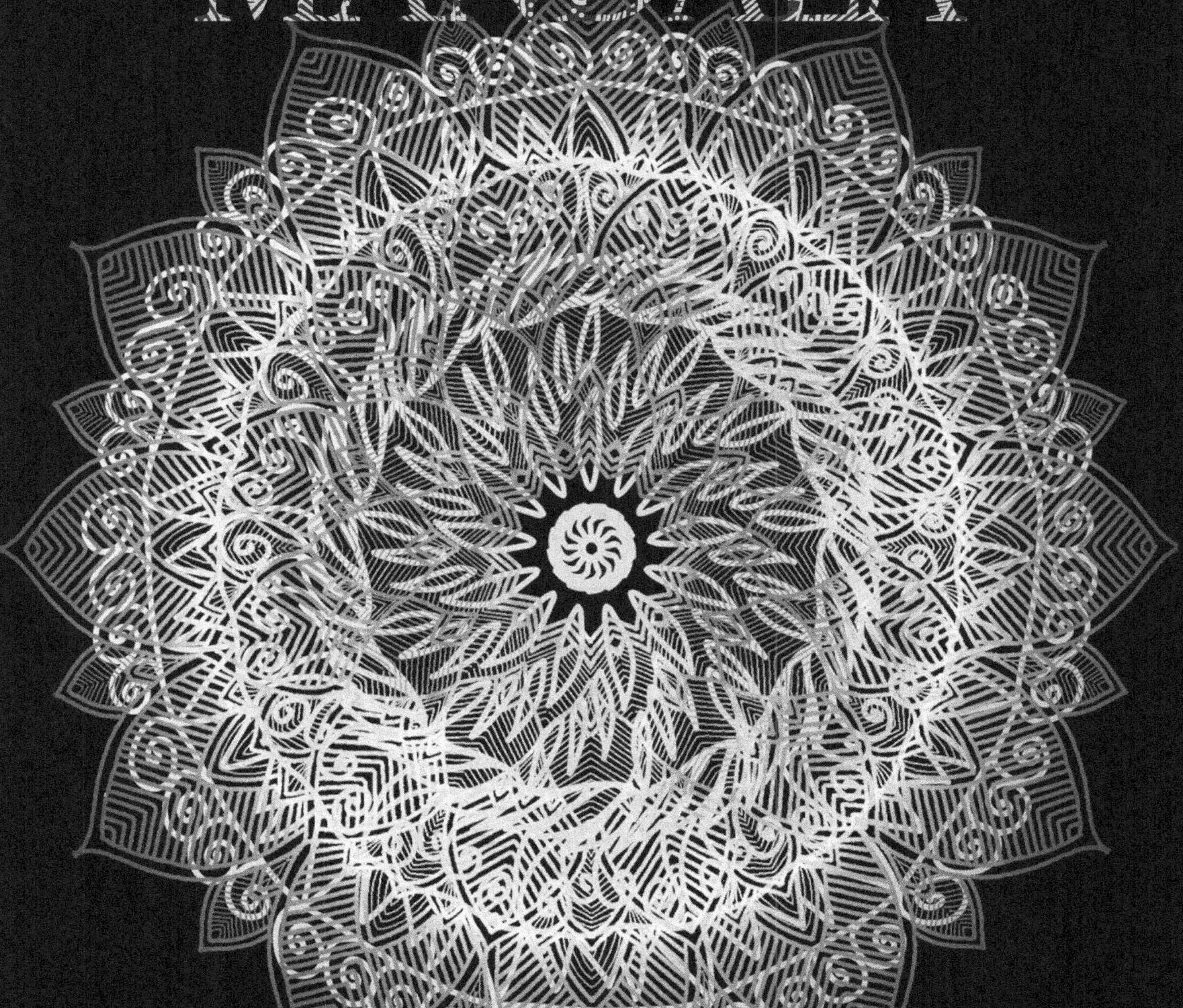

## Adult Coloring Book
## 50 Mandalas
## For Relax and Anti-Stress

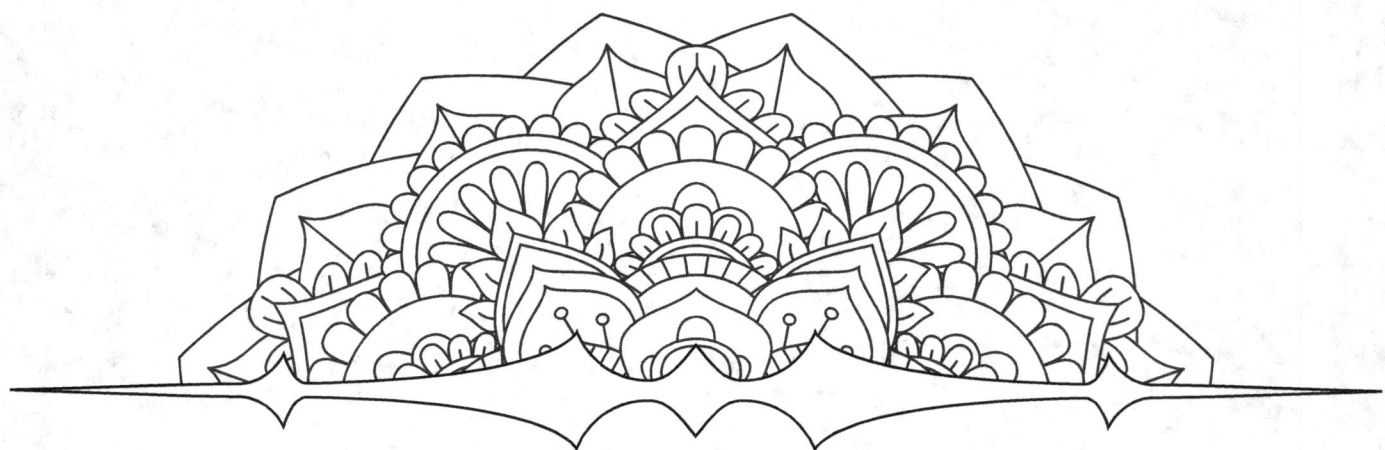

# THIS BOOK
## Belongs to:
_____
_____

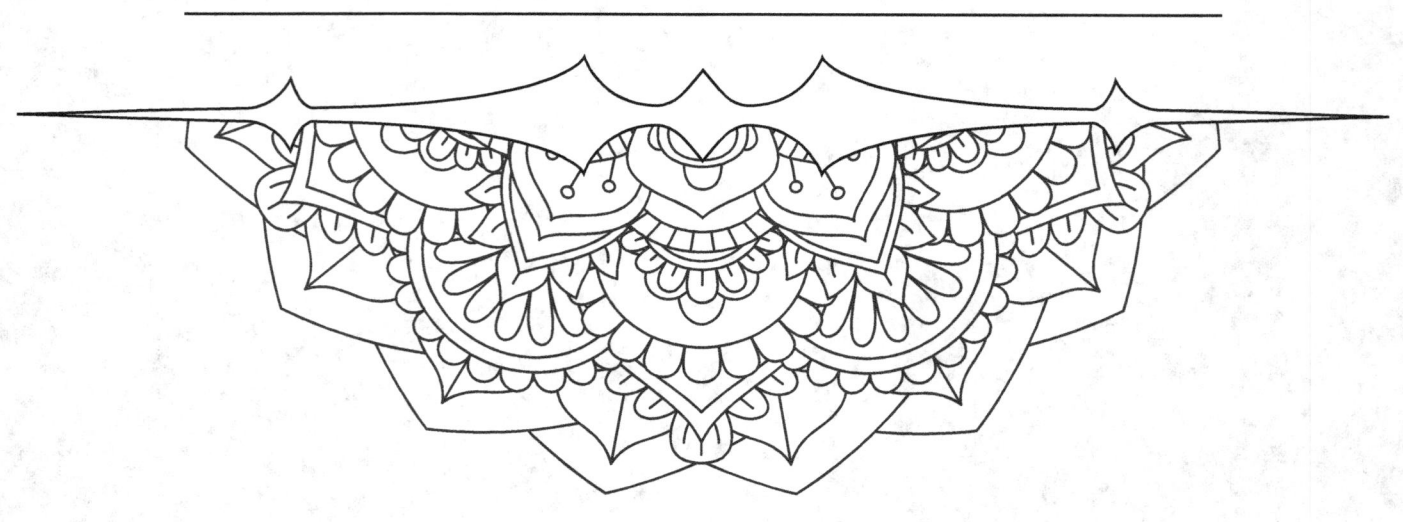

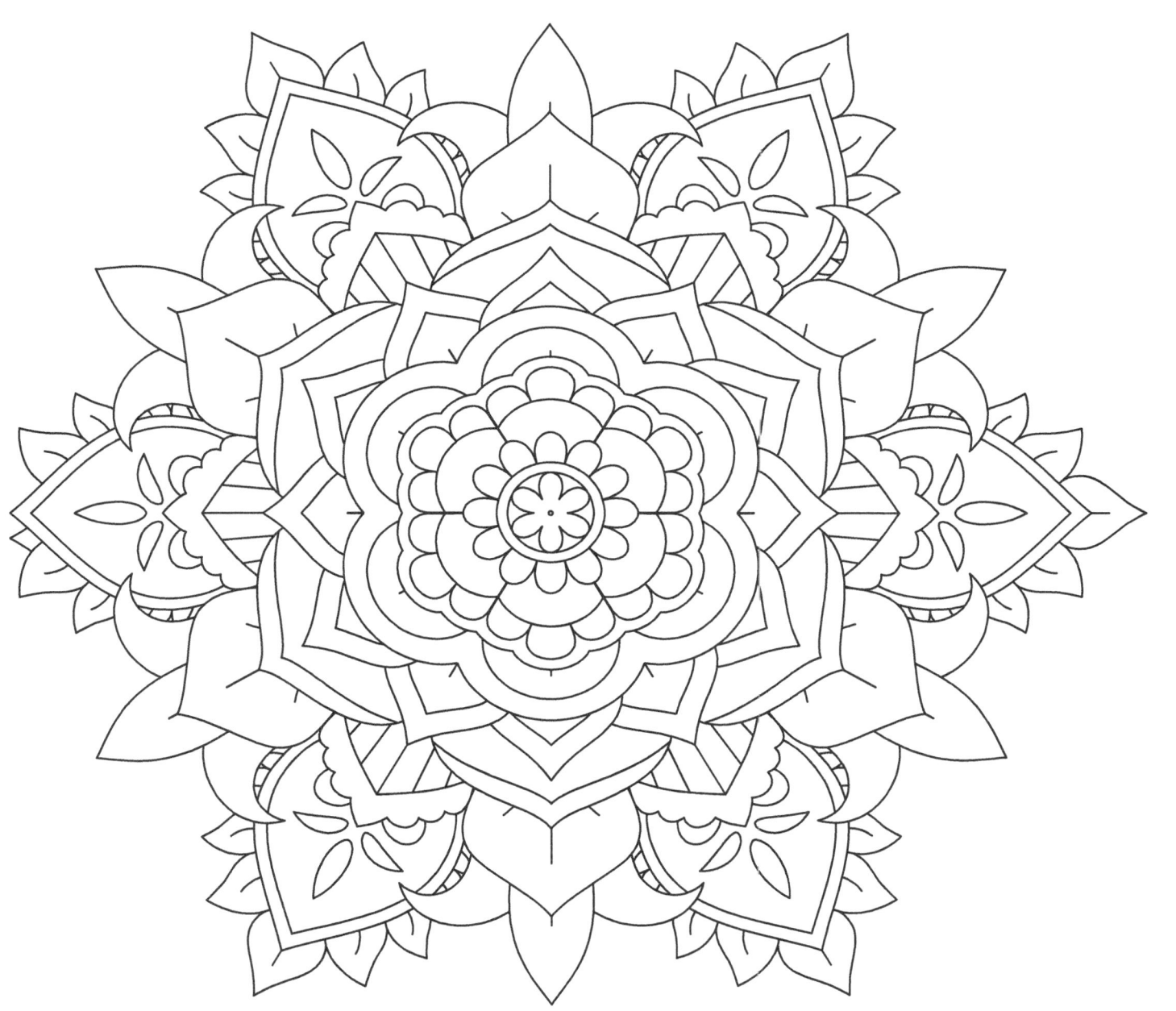

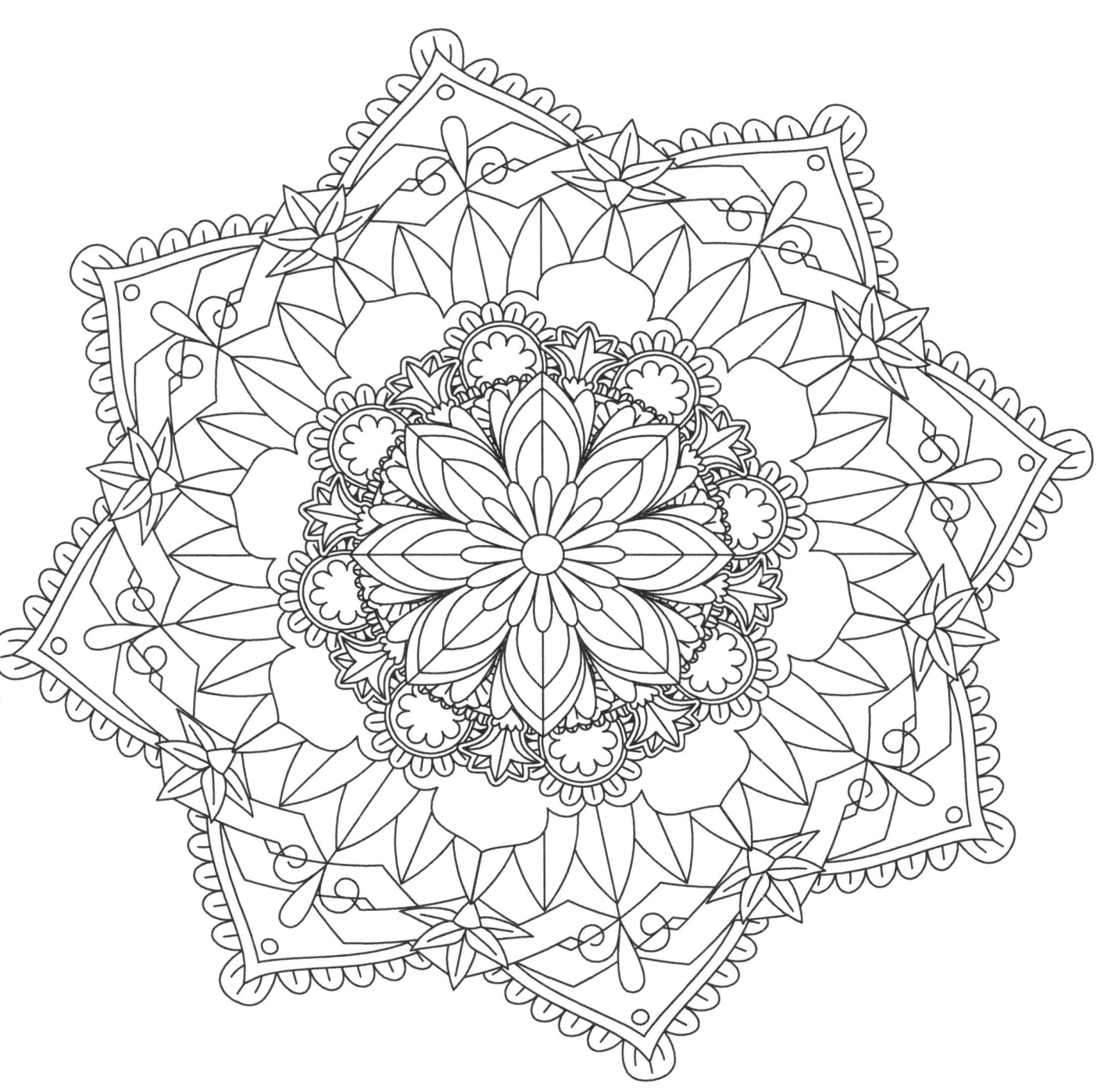

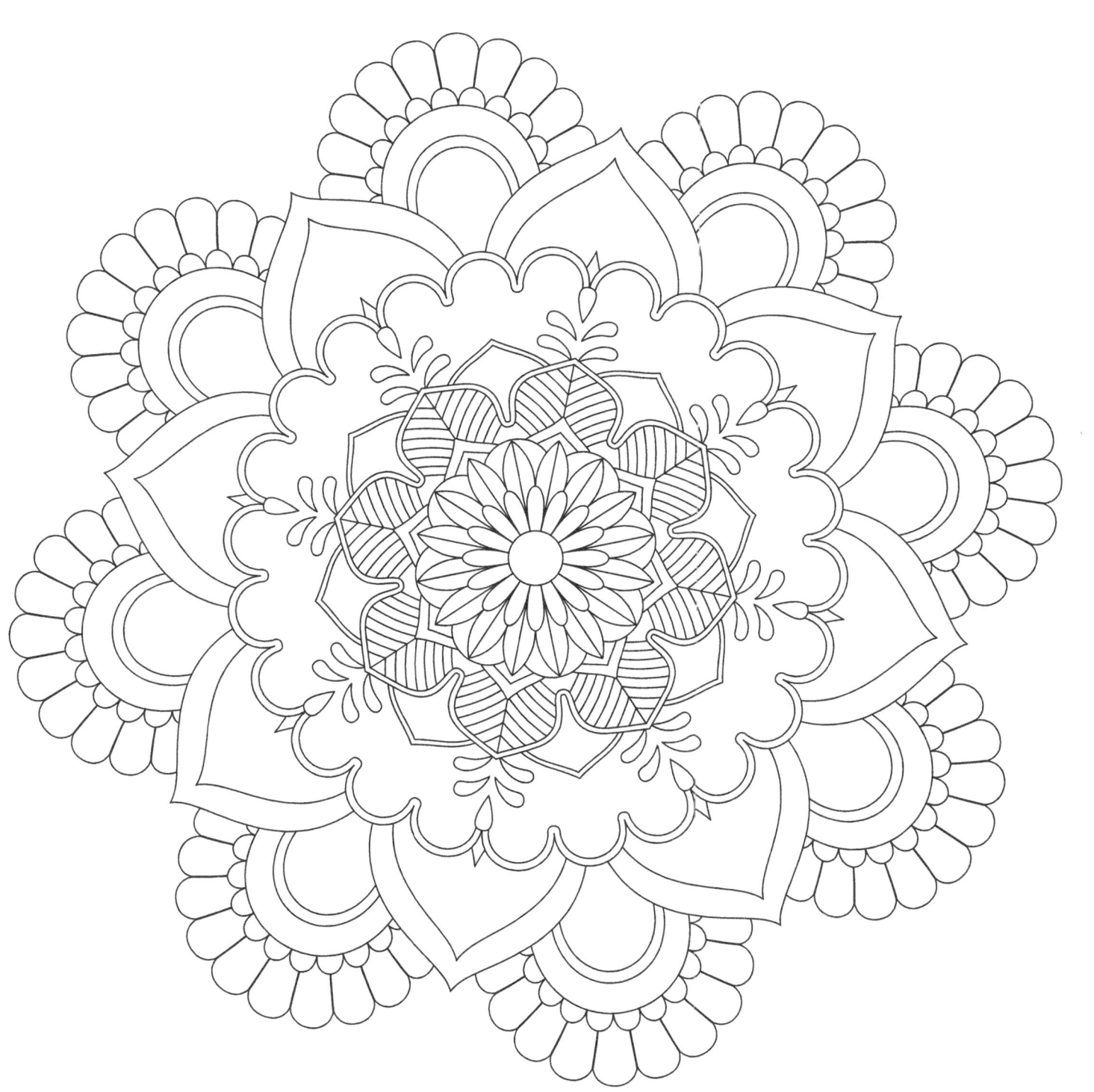

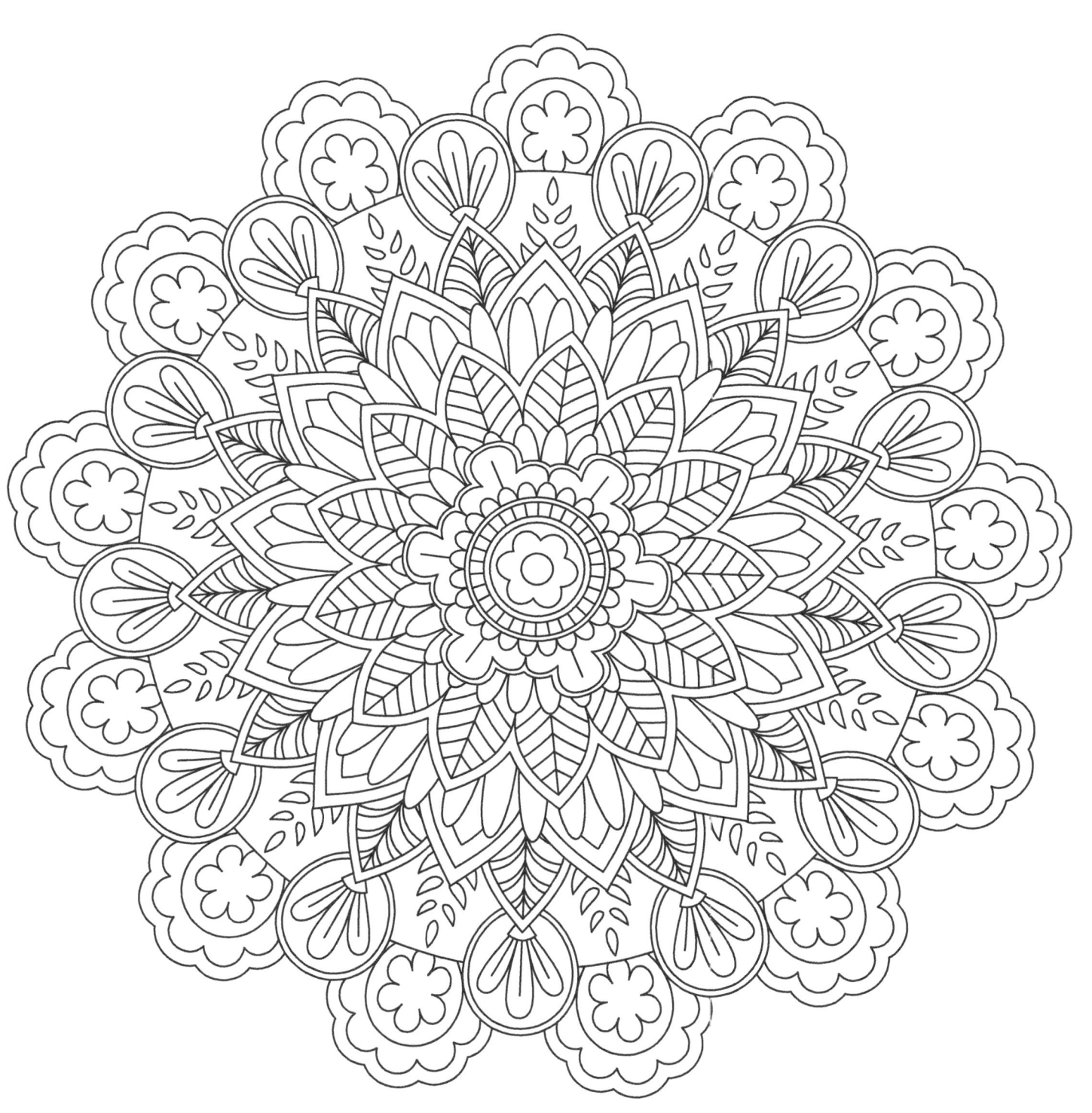

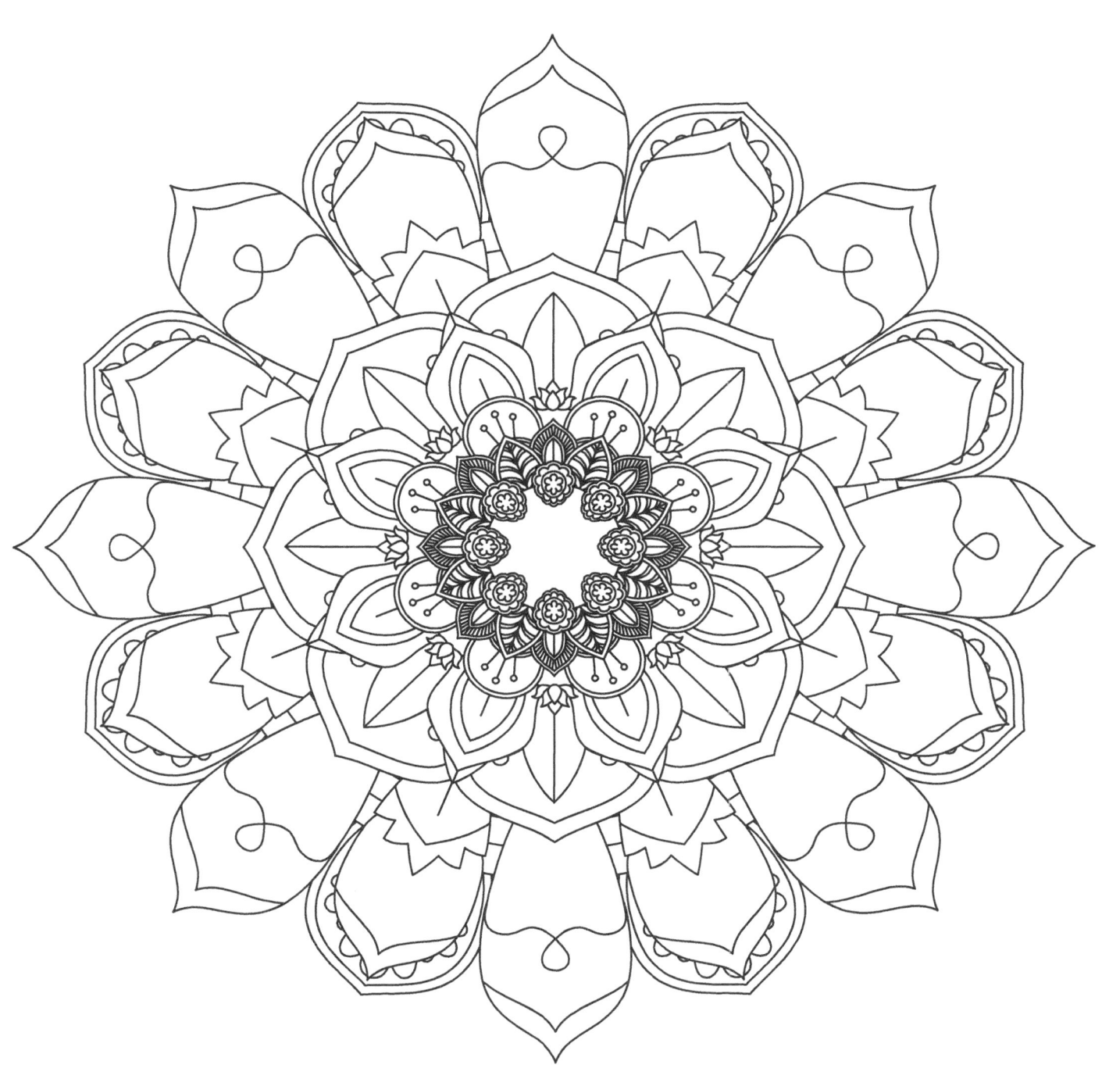

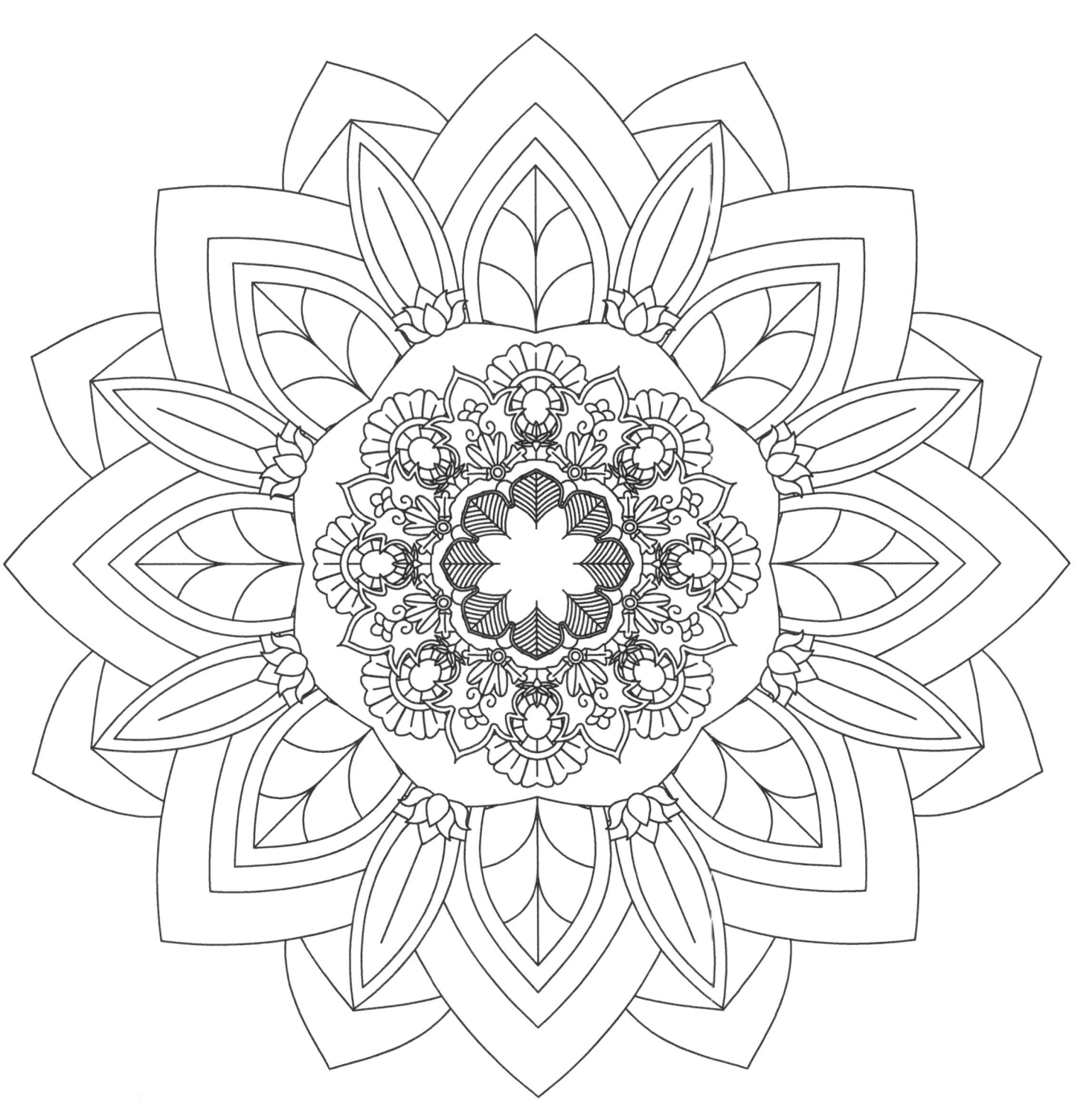

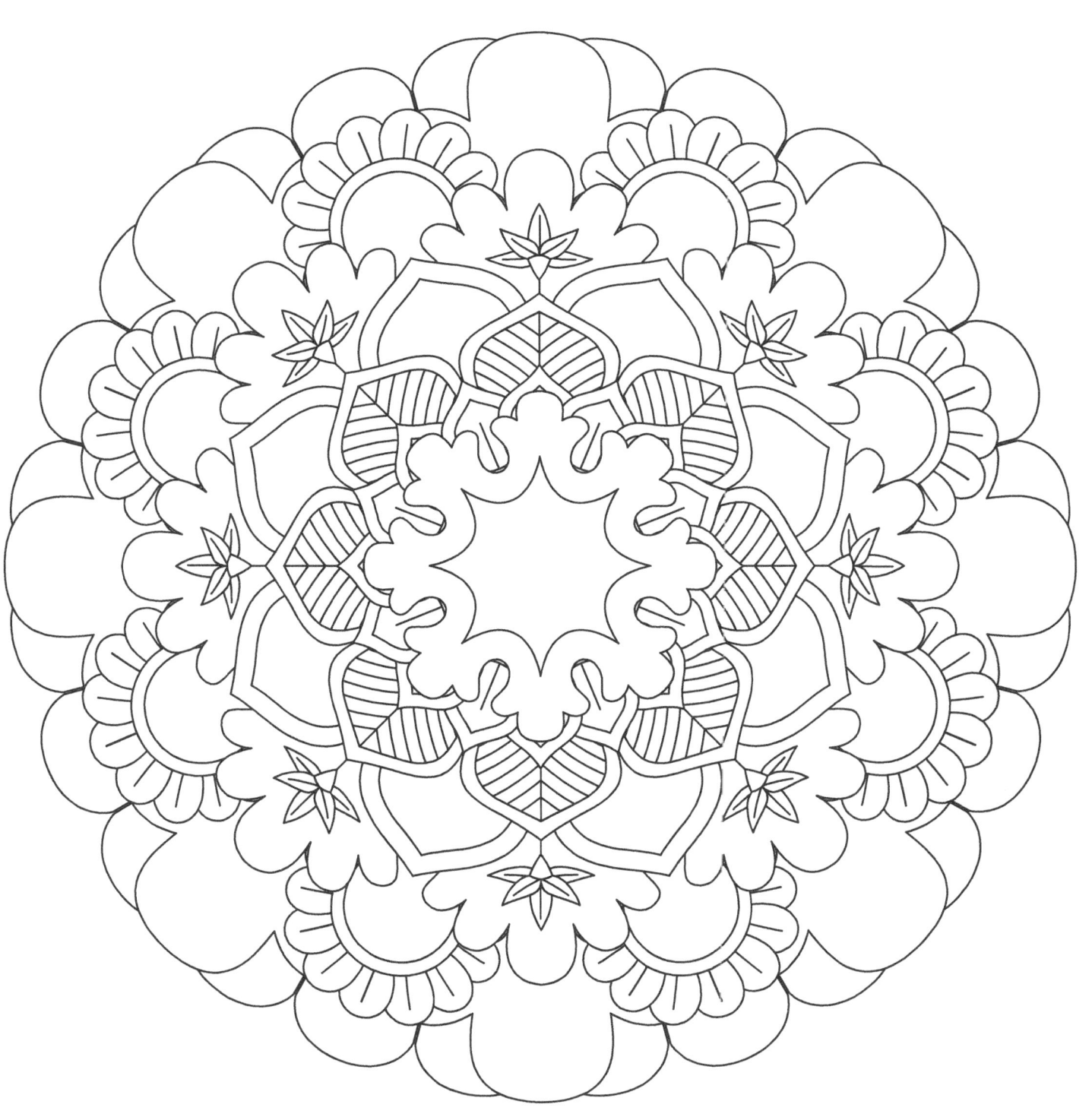

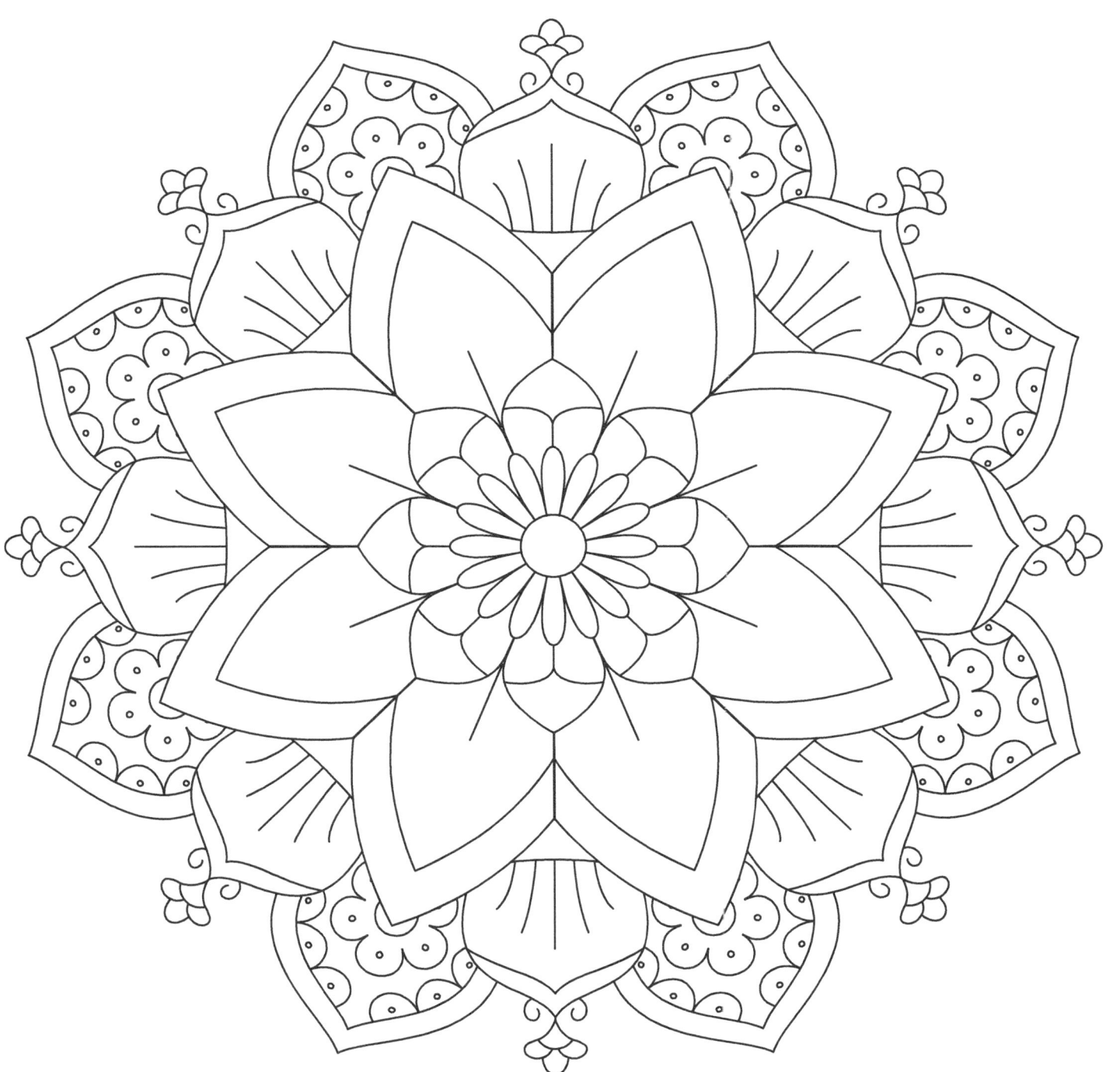

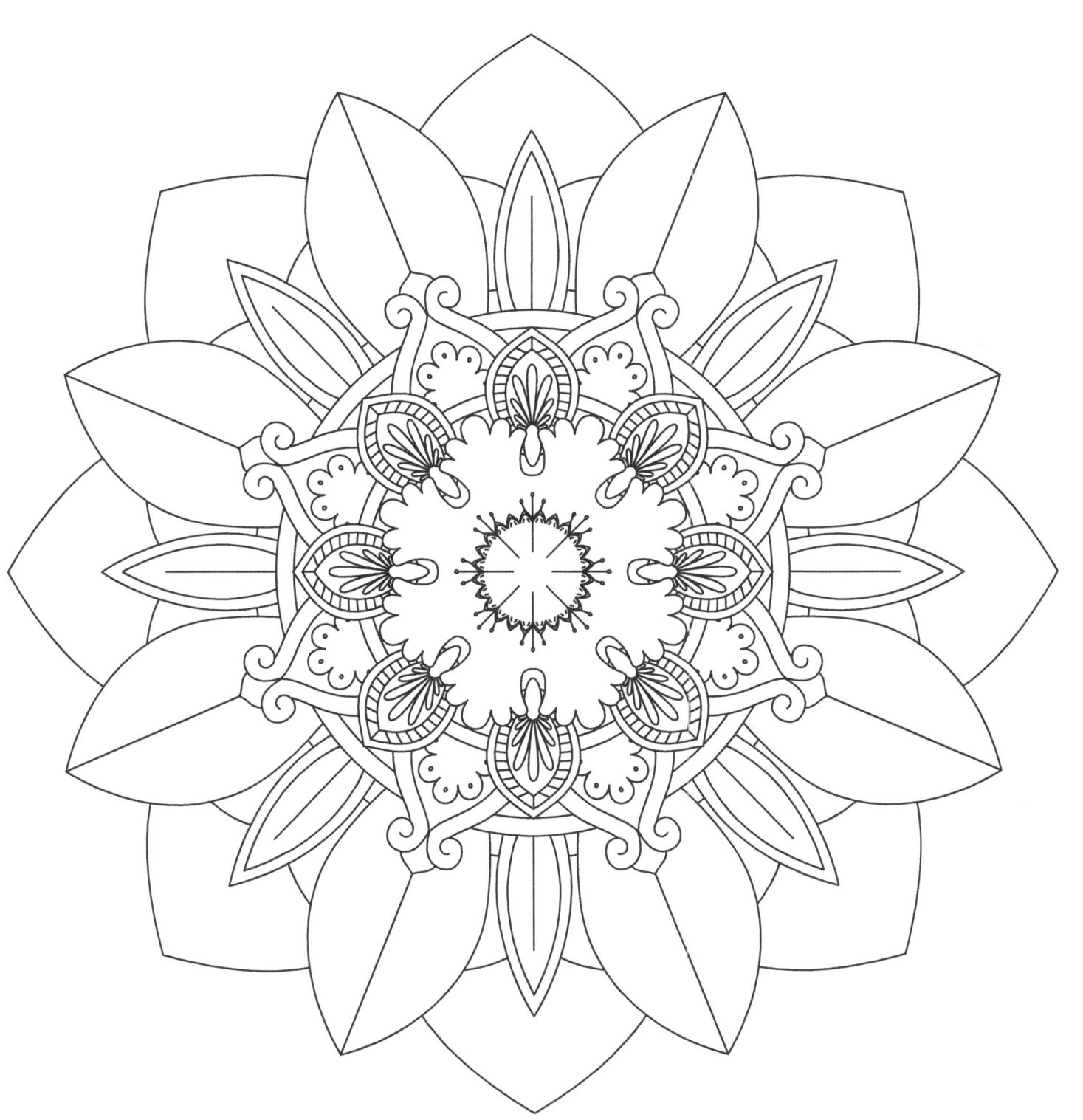

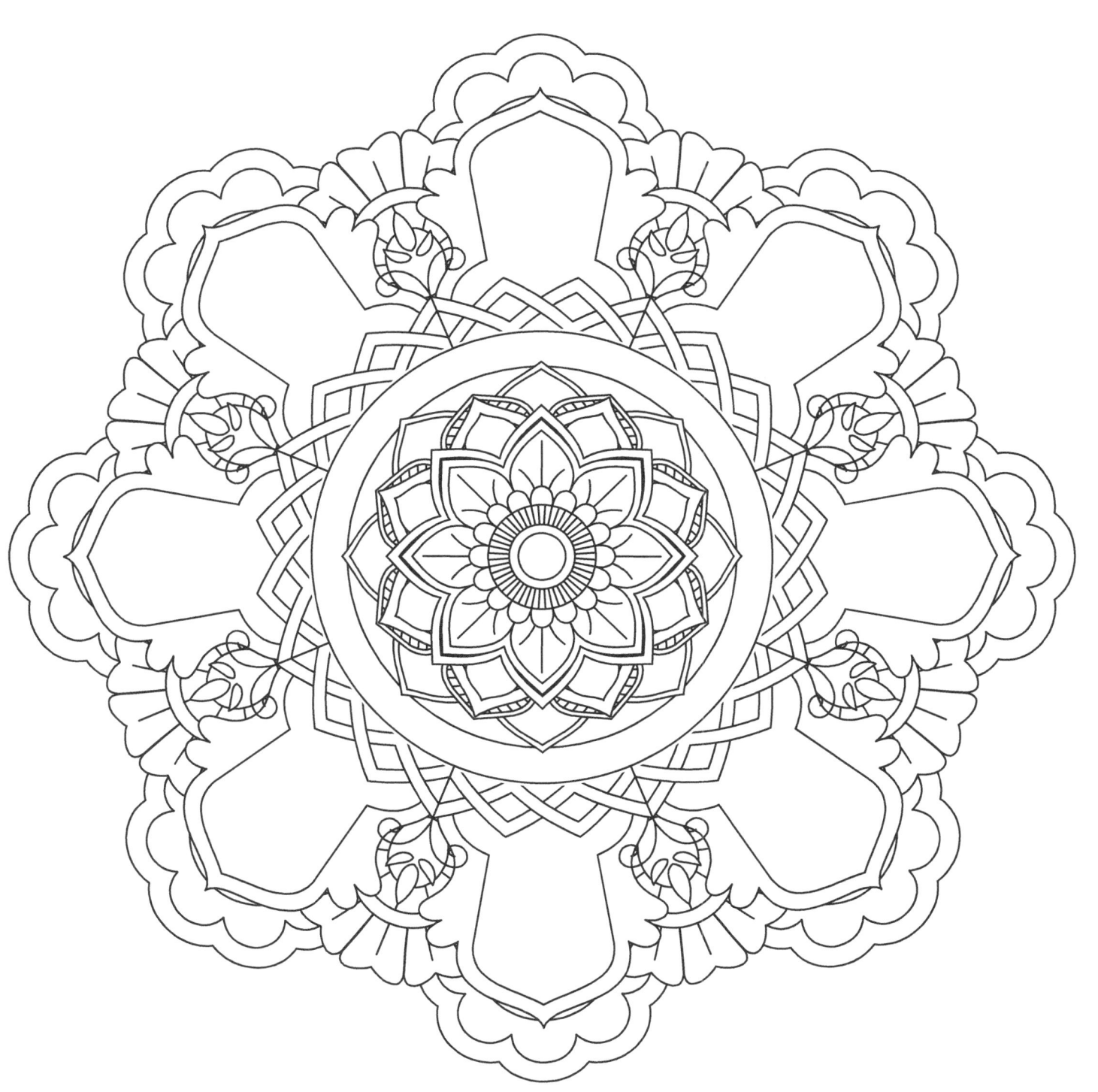

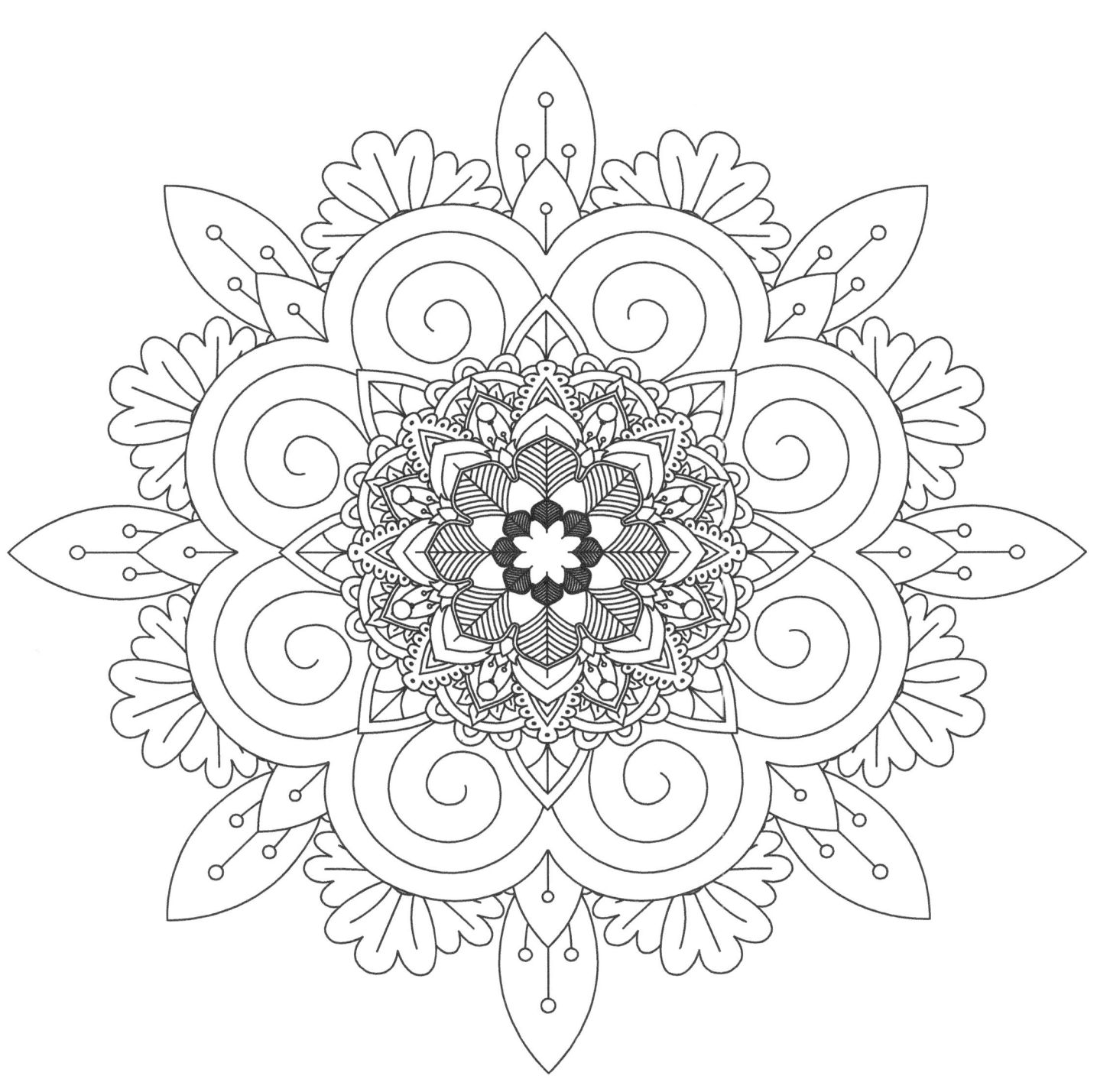

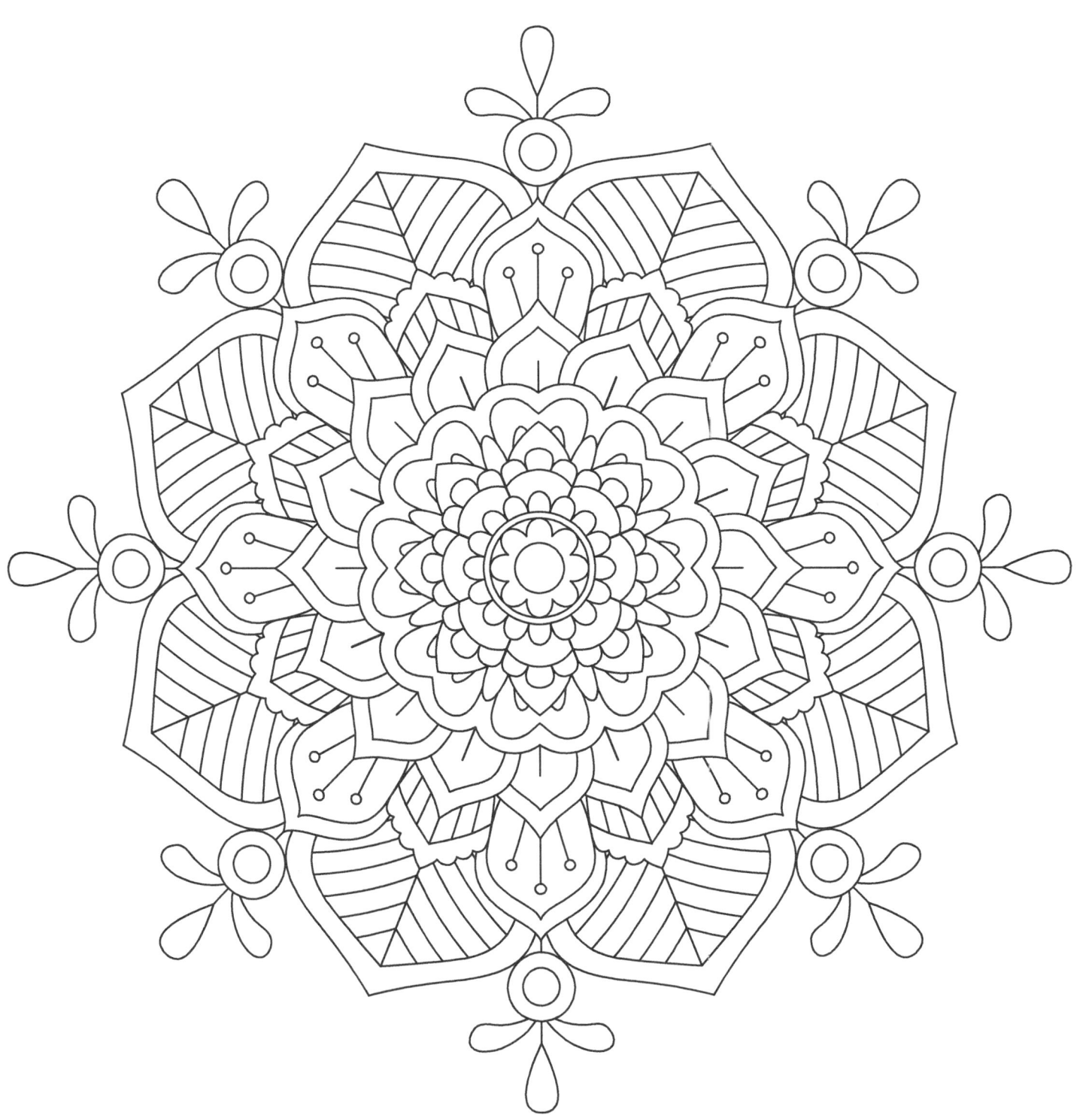

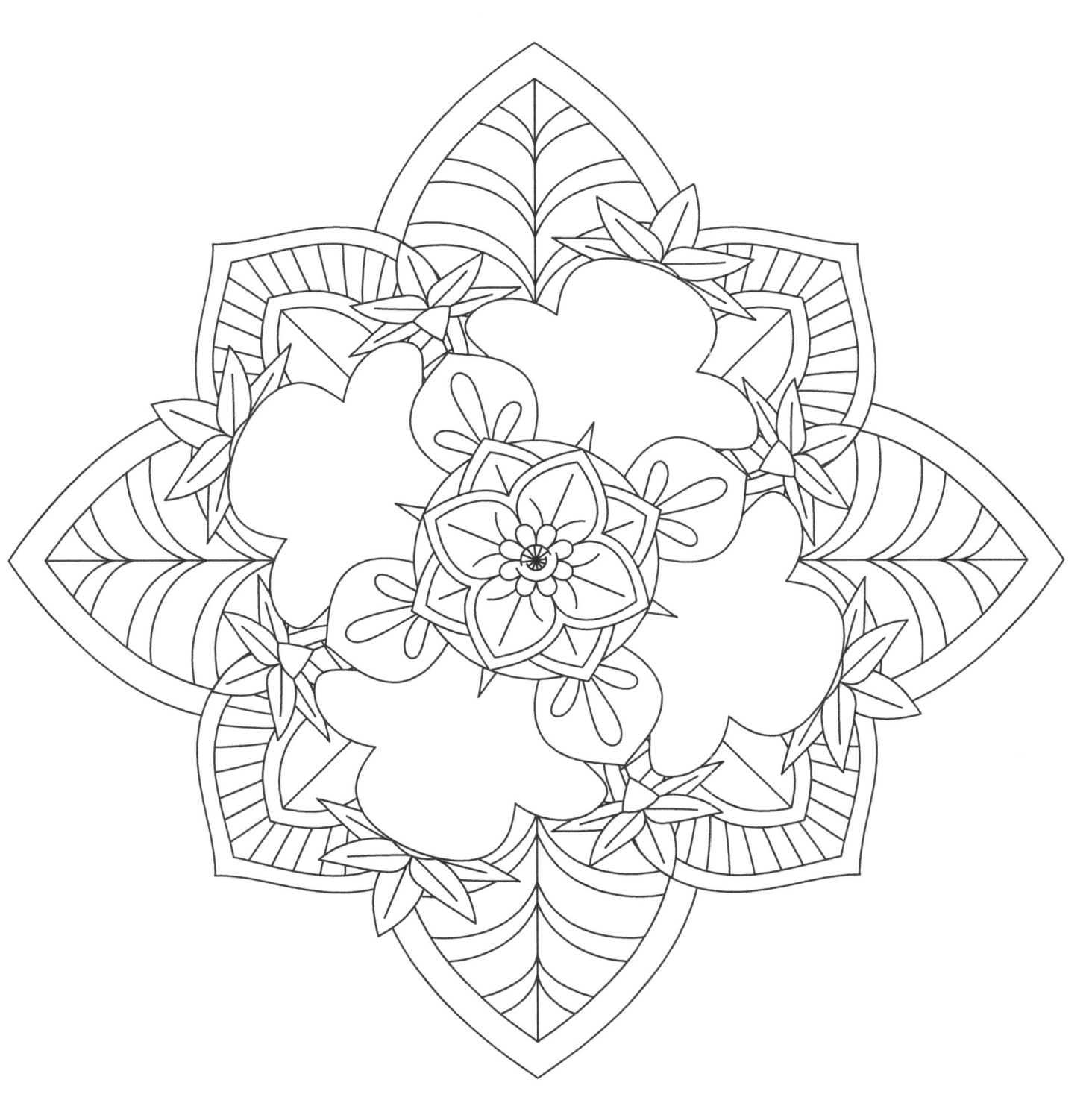

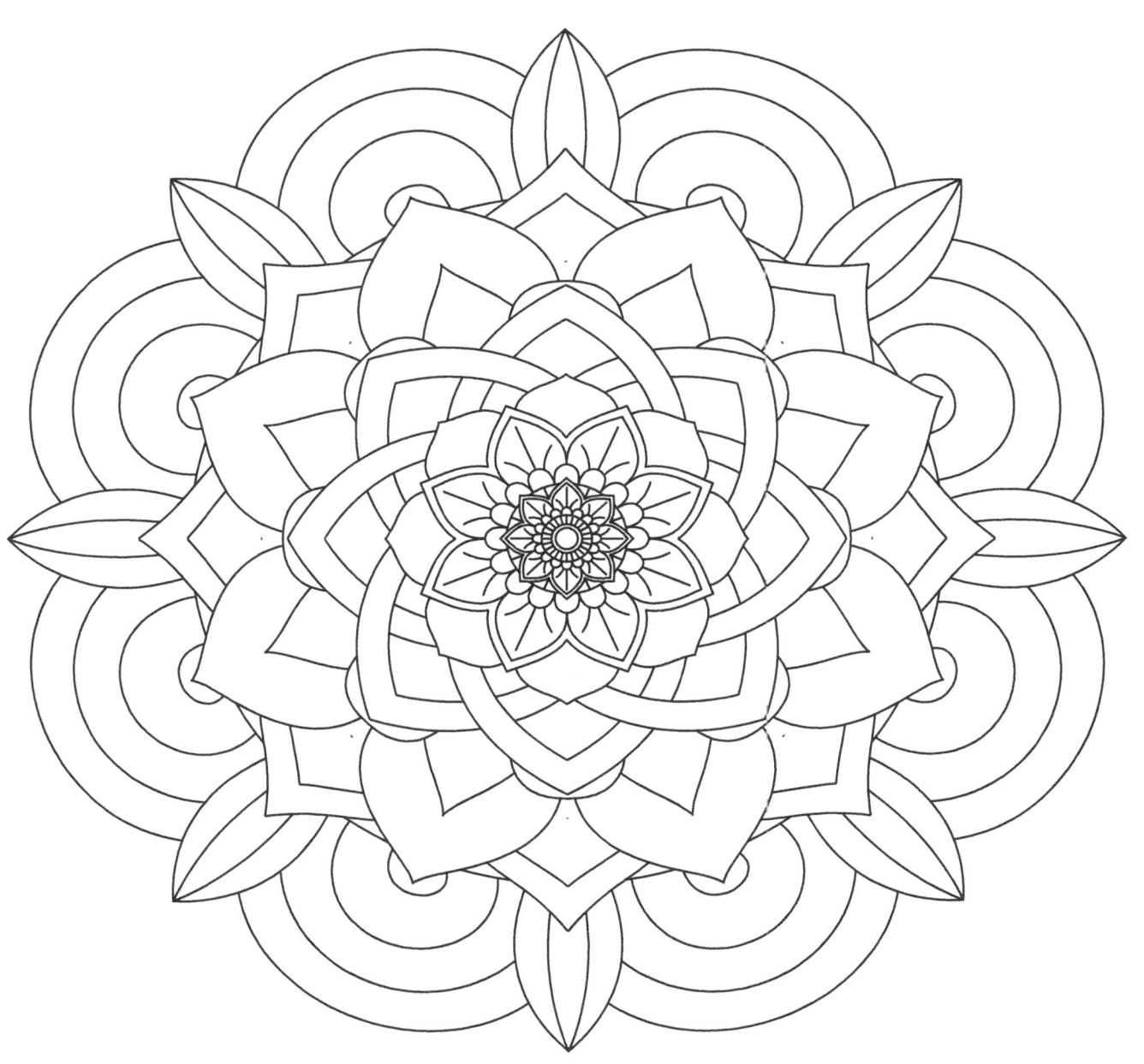

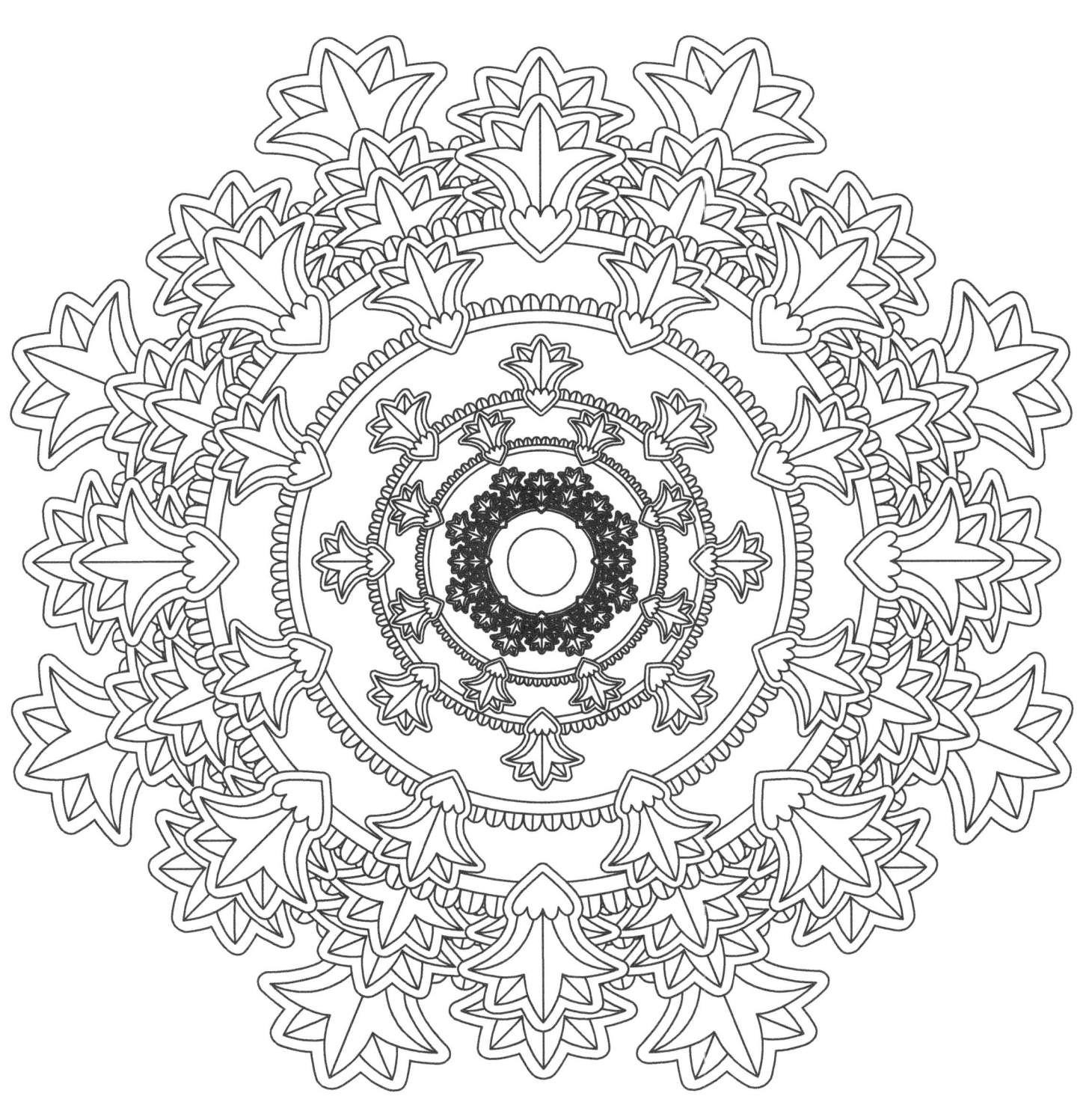

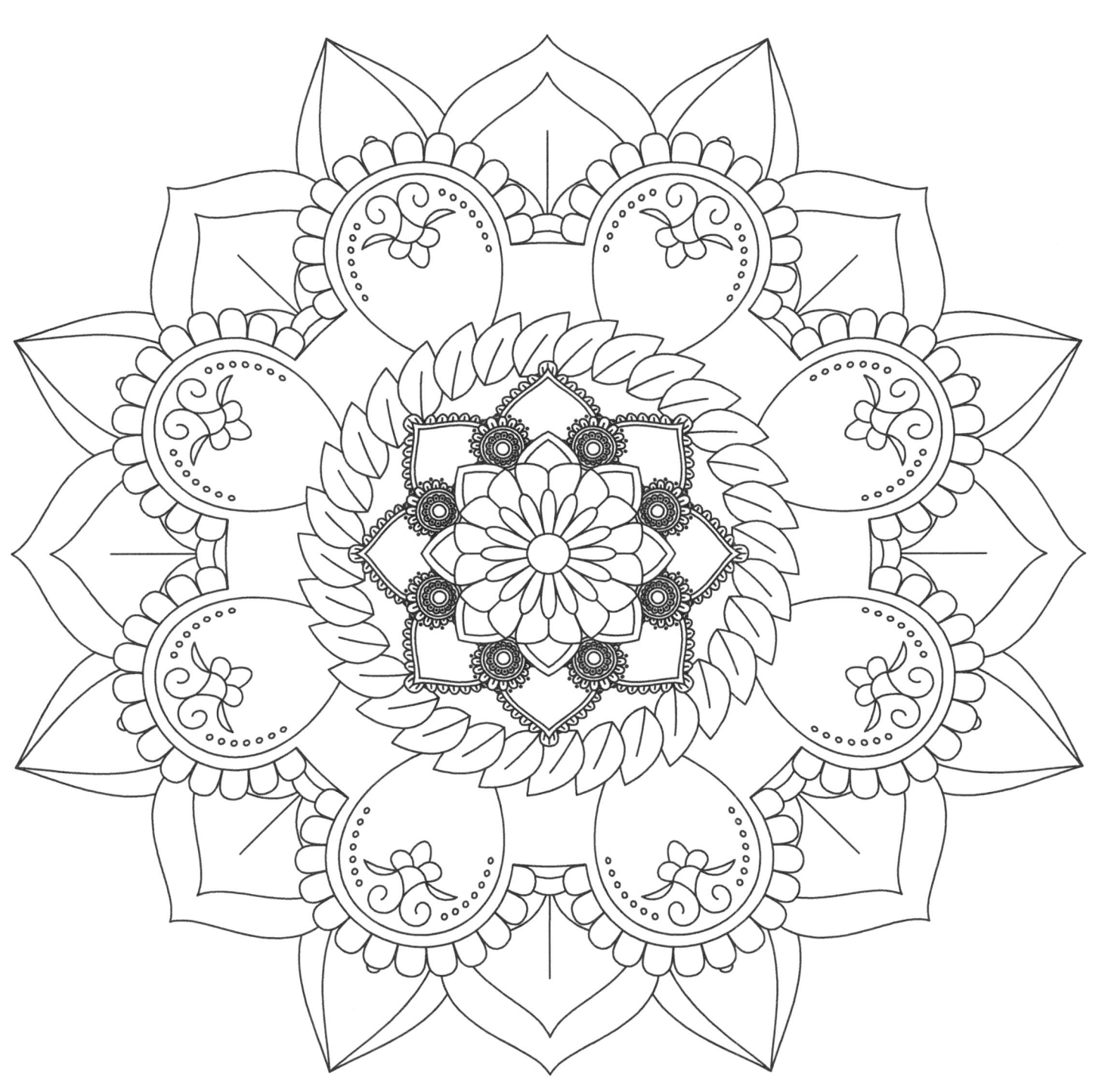

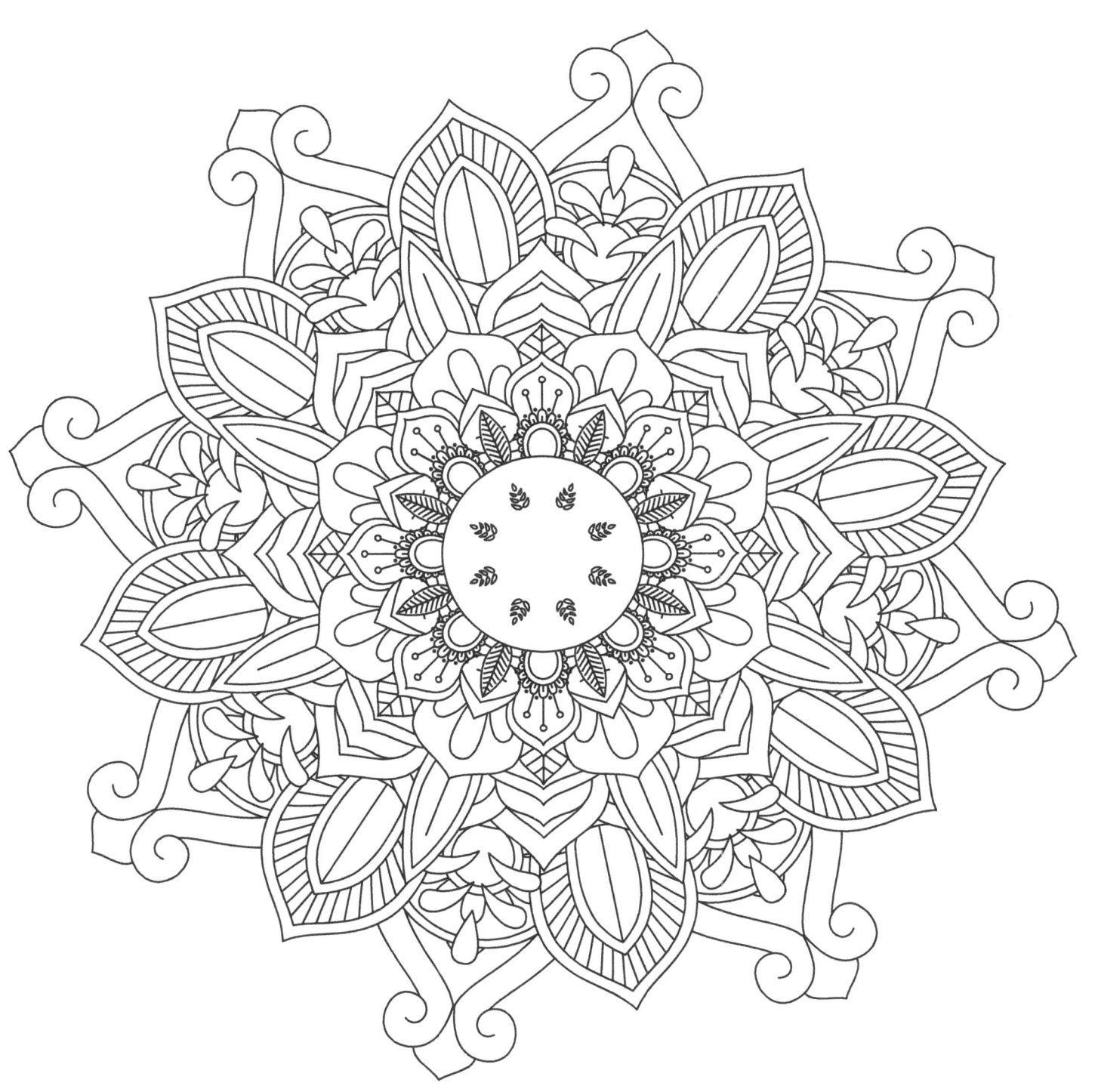

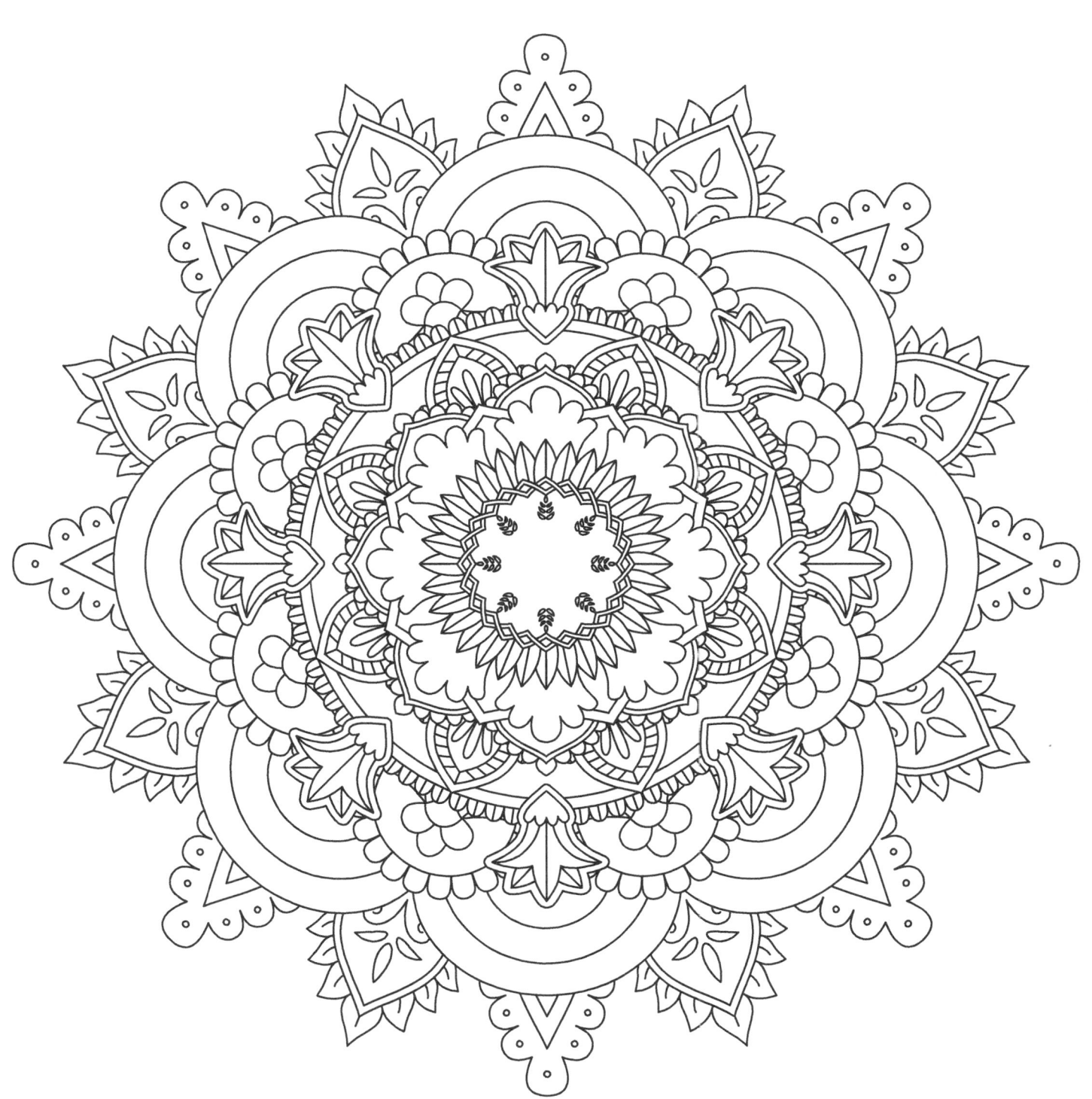

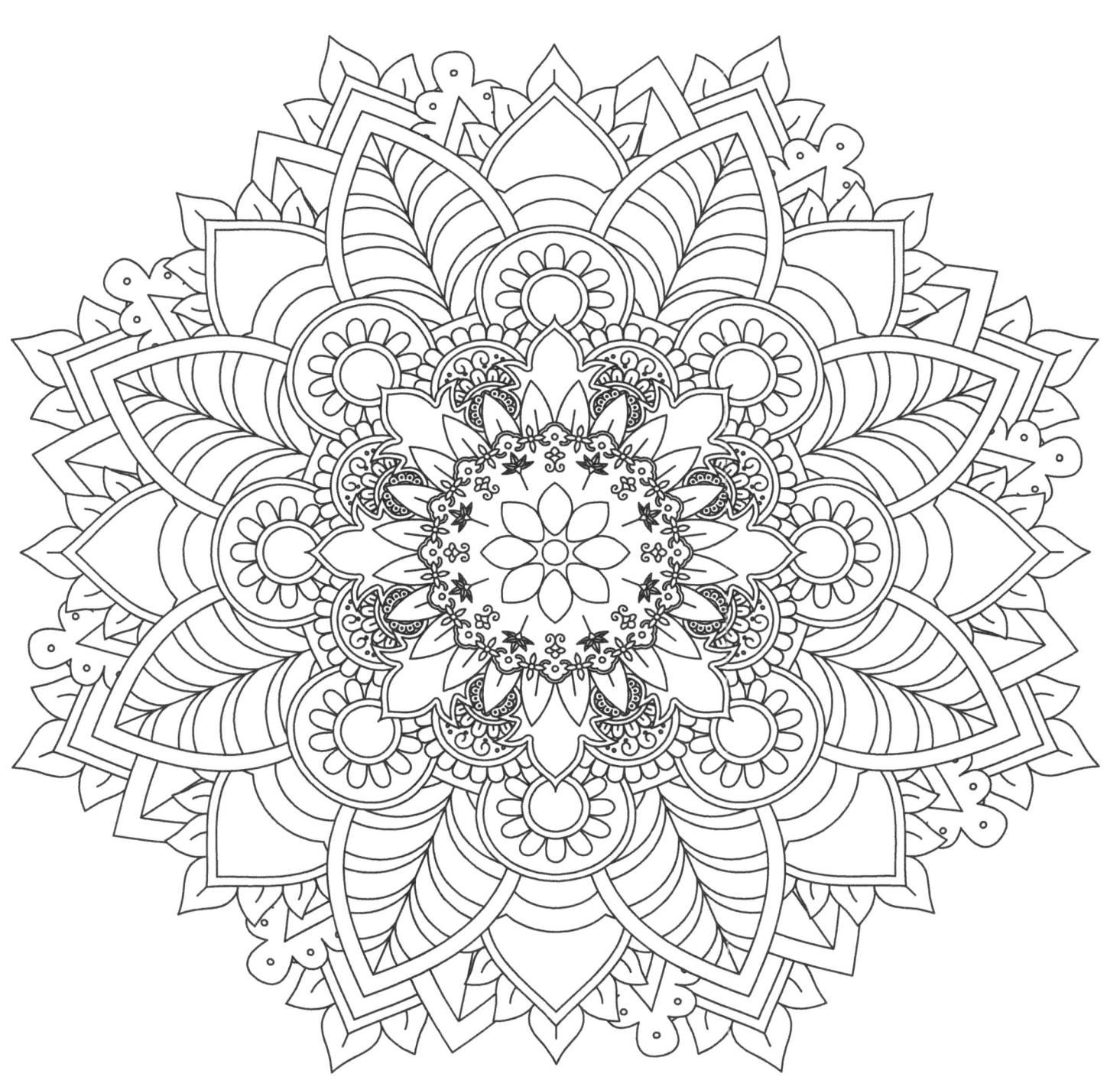

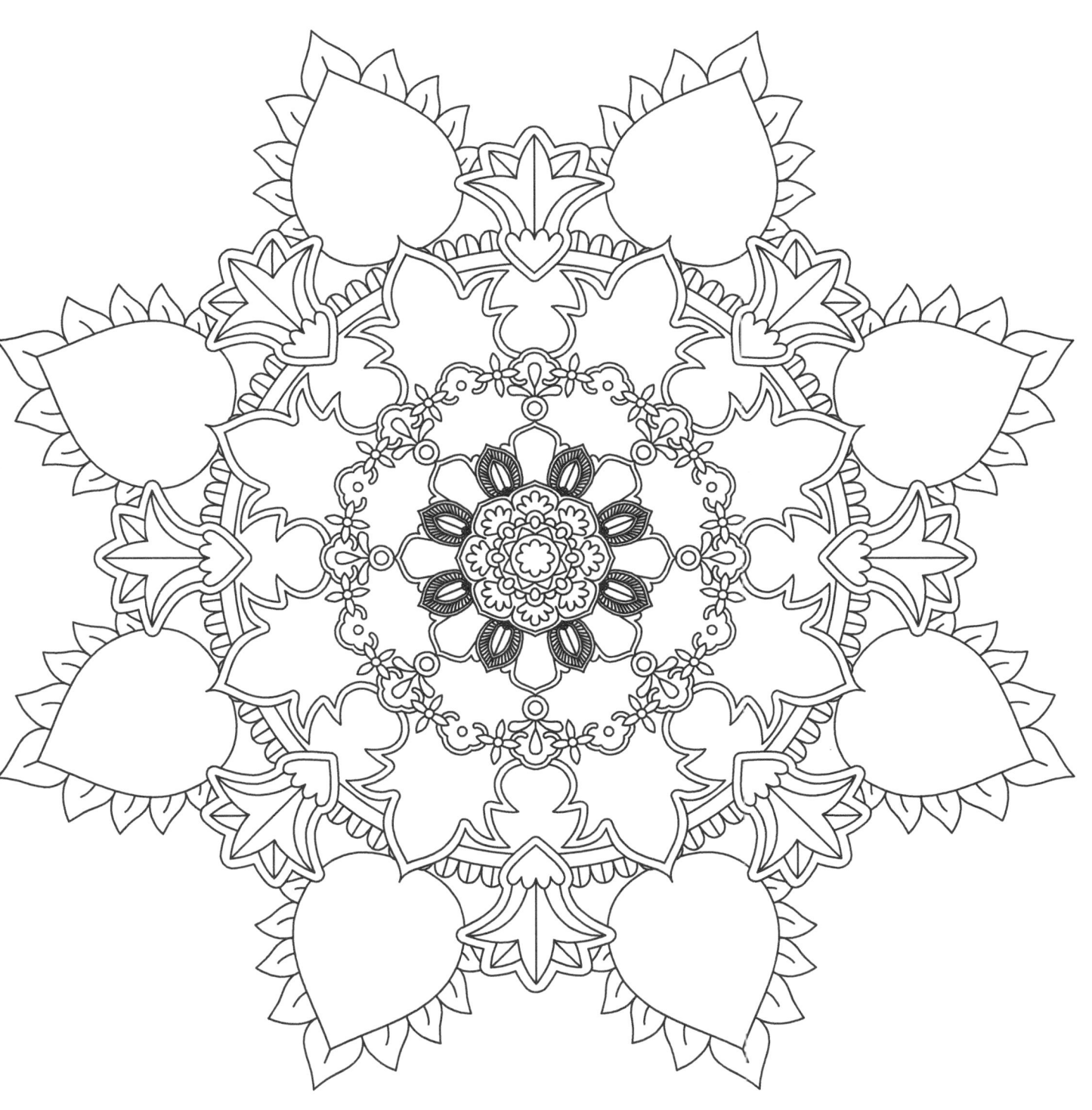

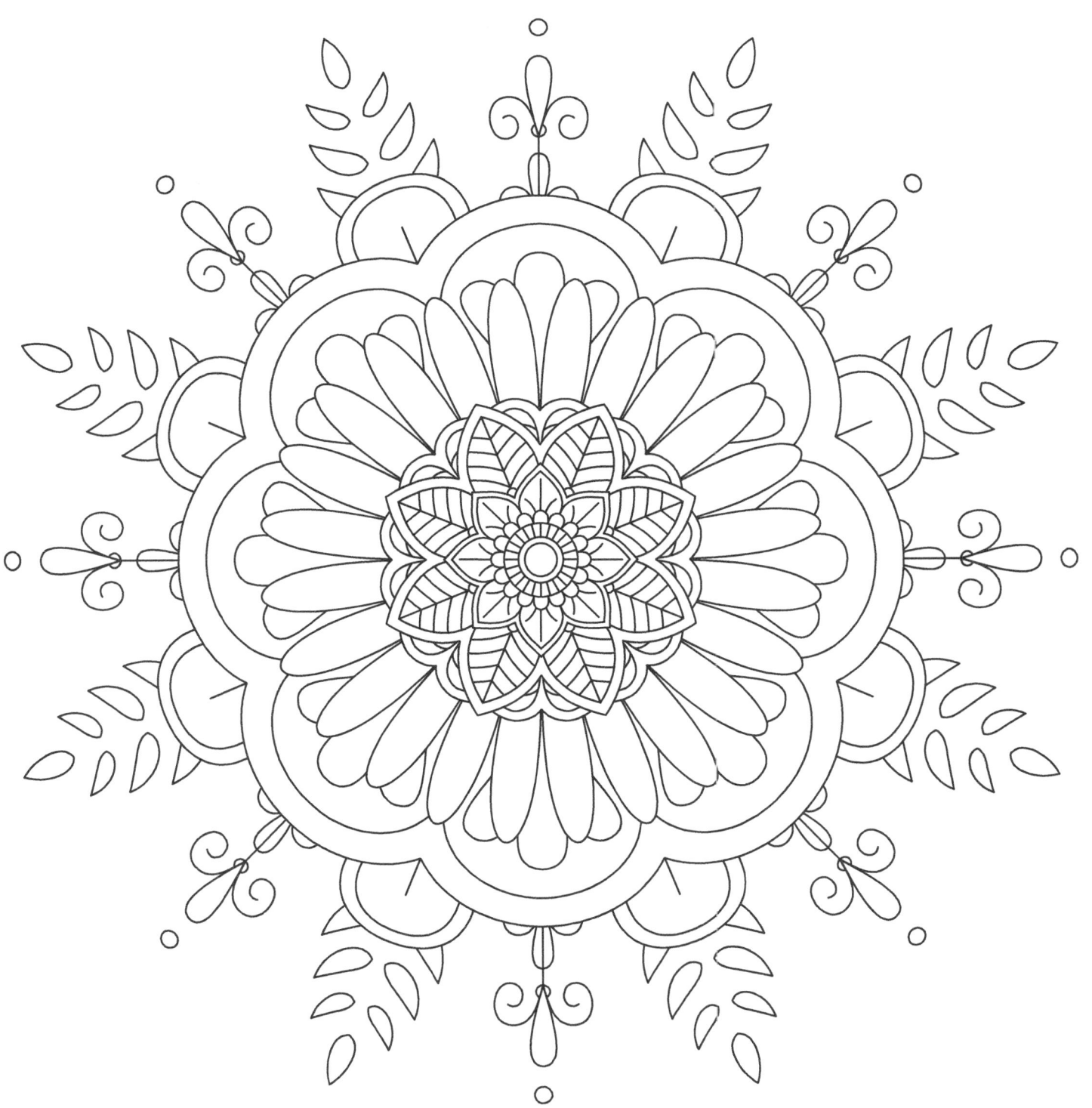

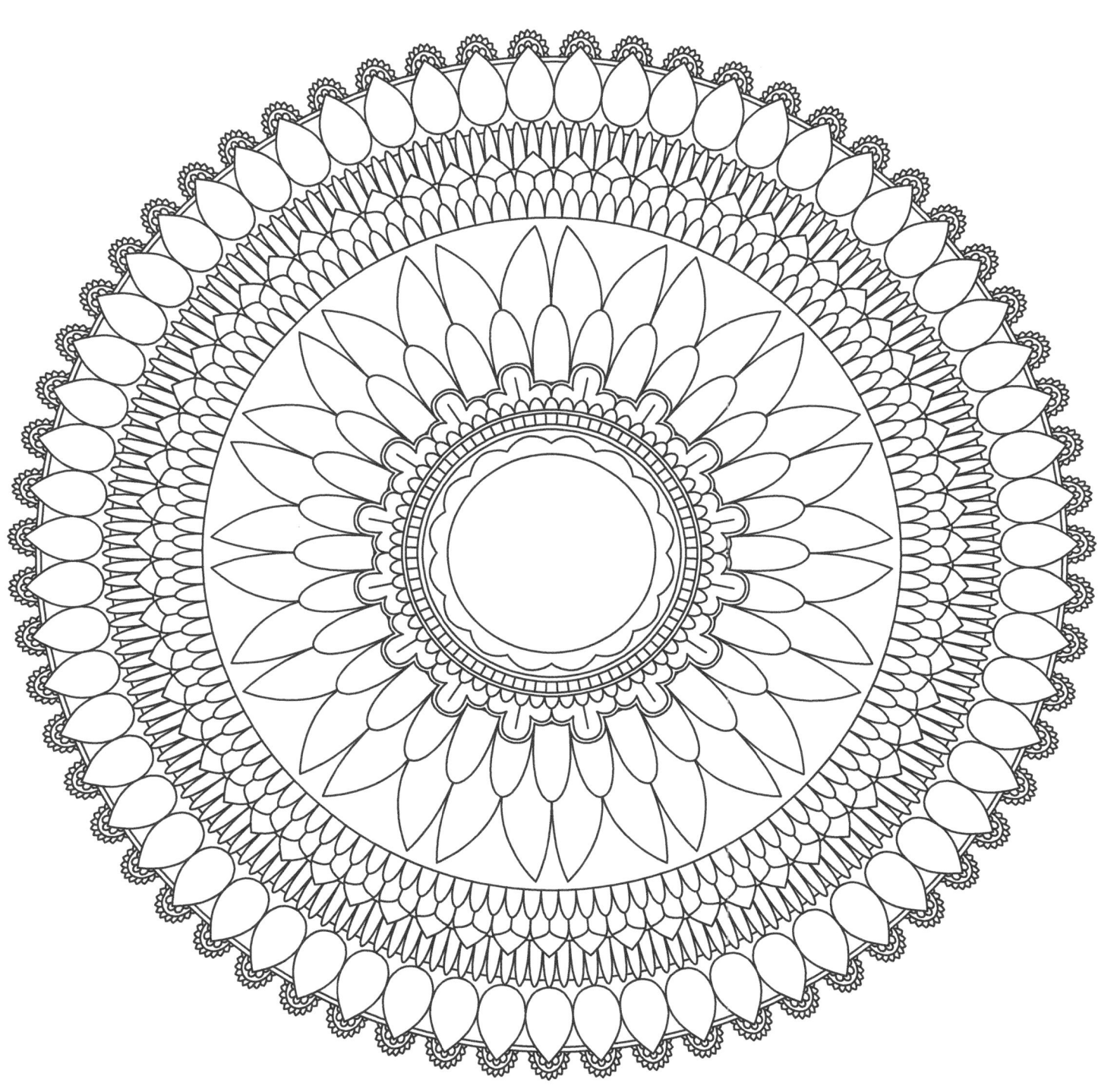

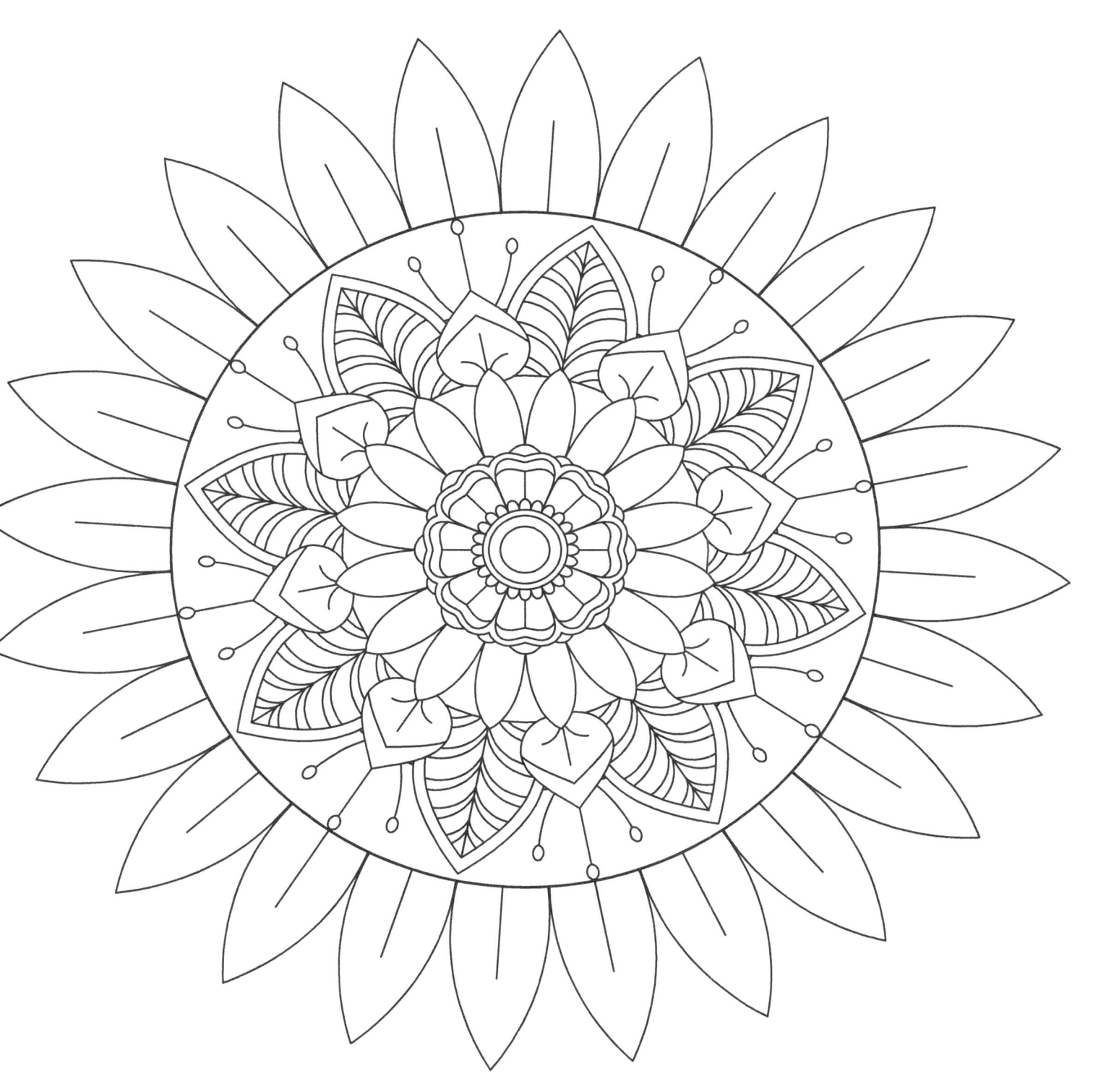

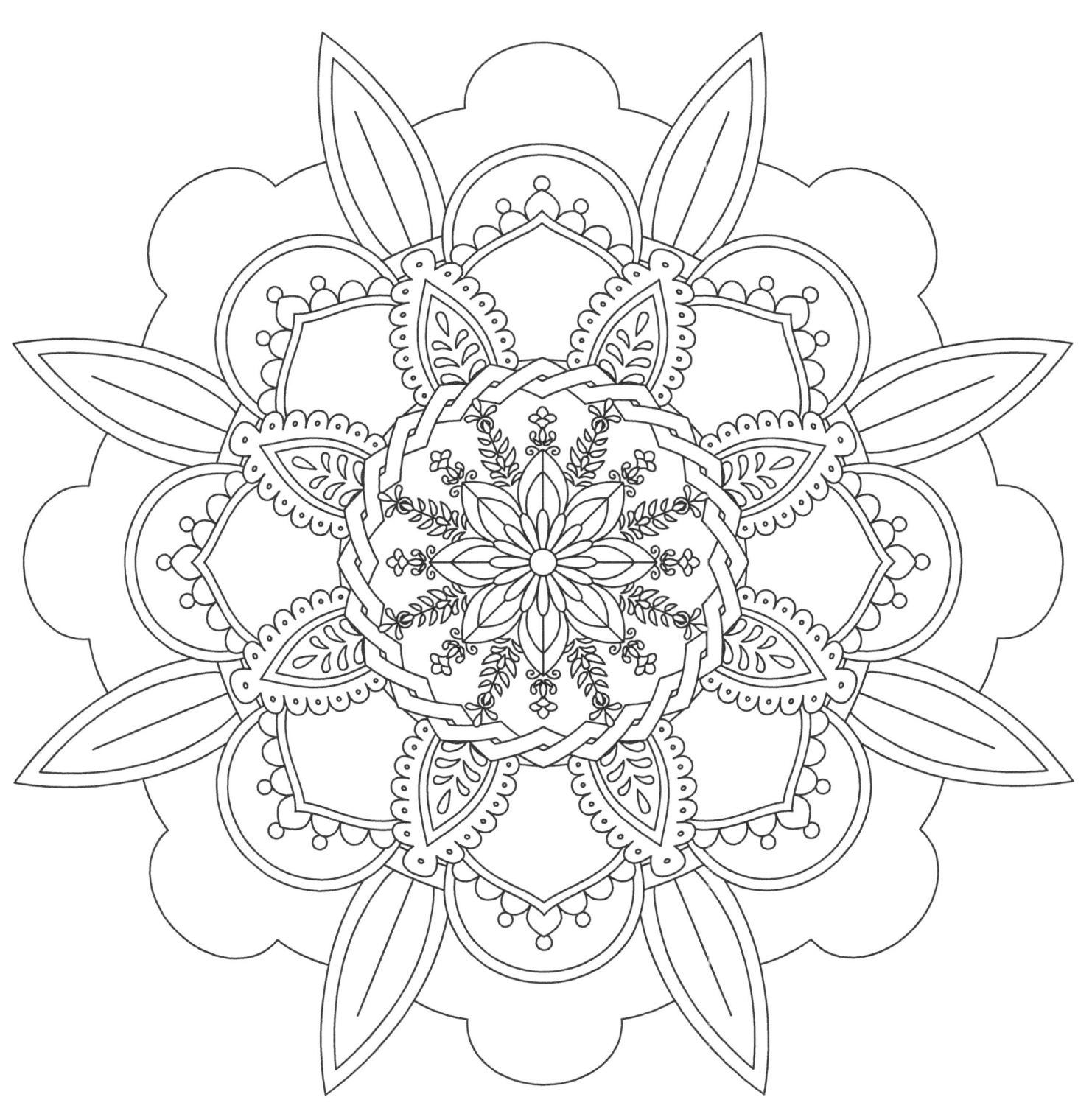

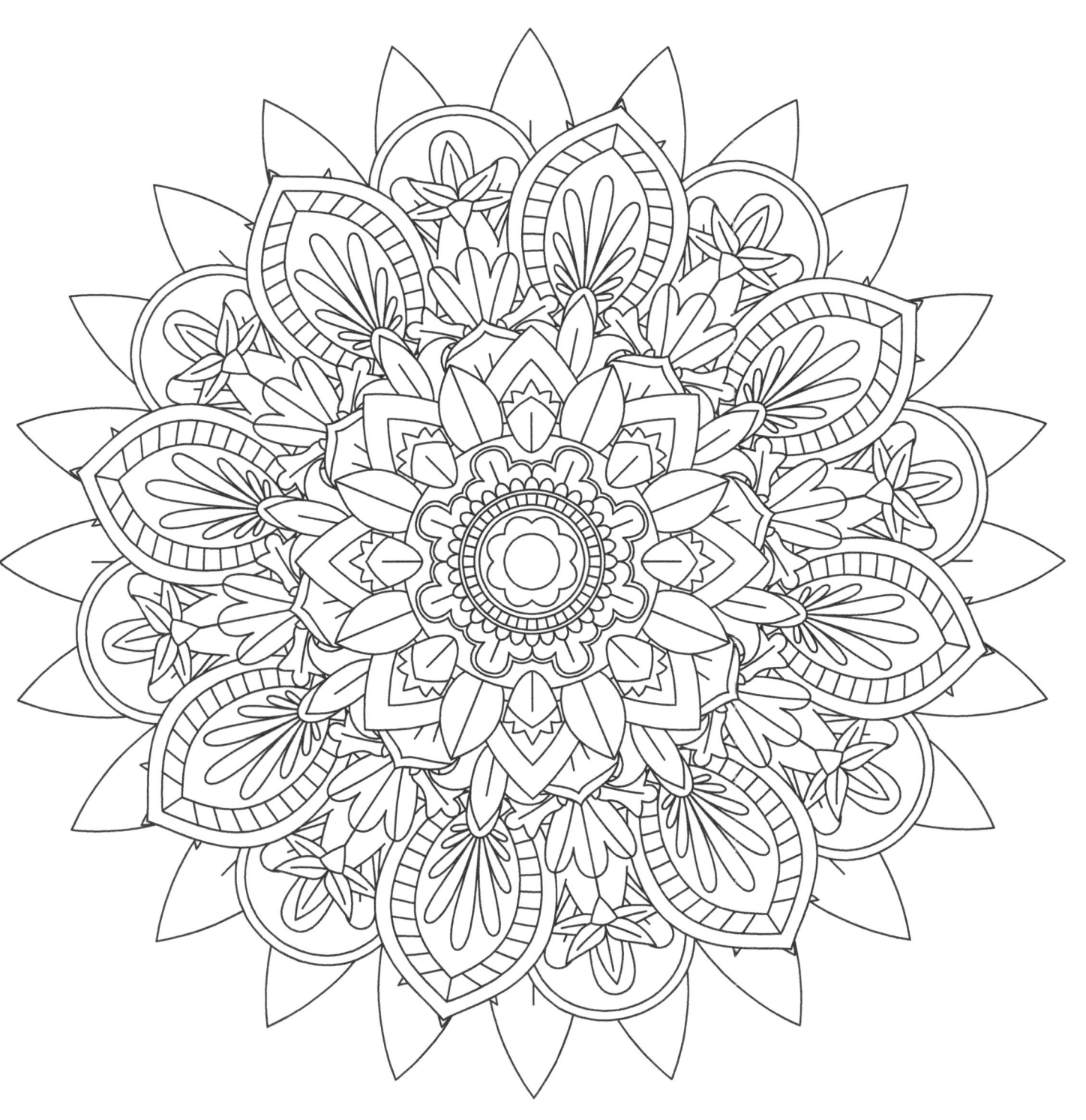

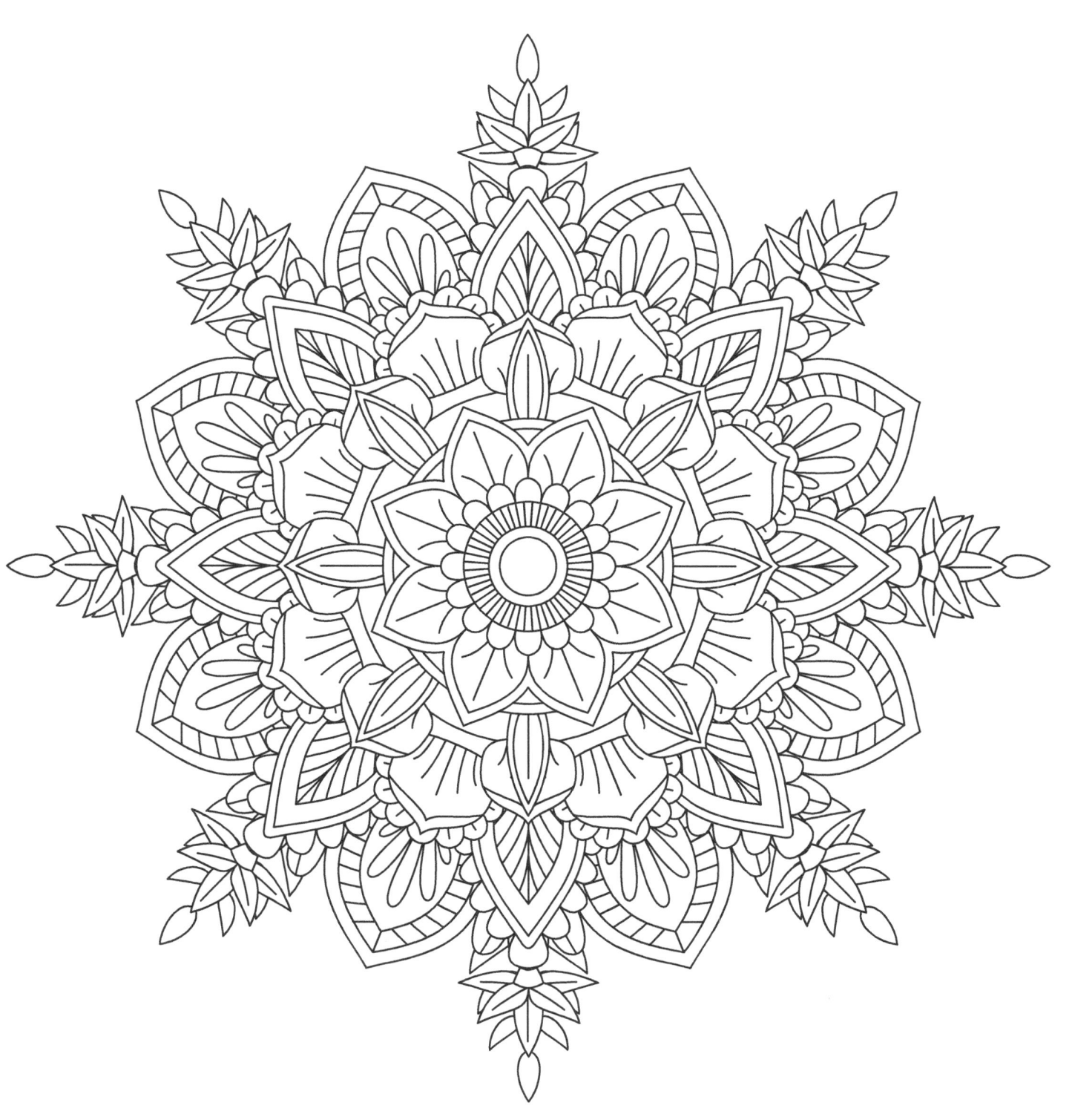

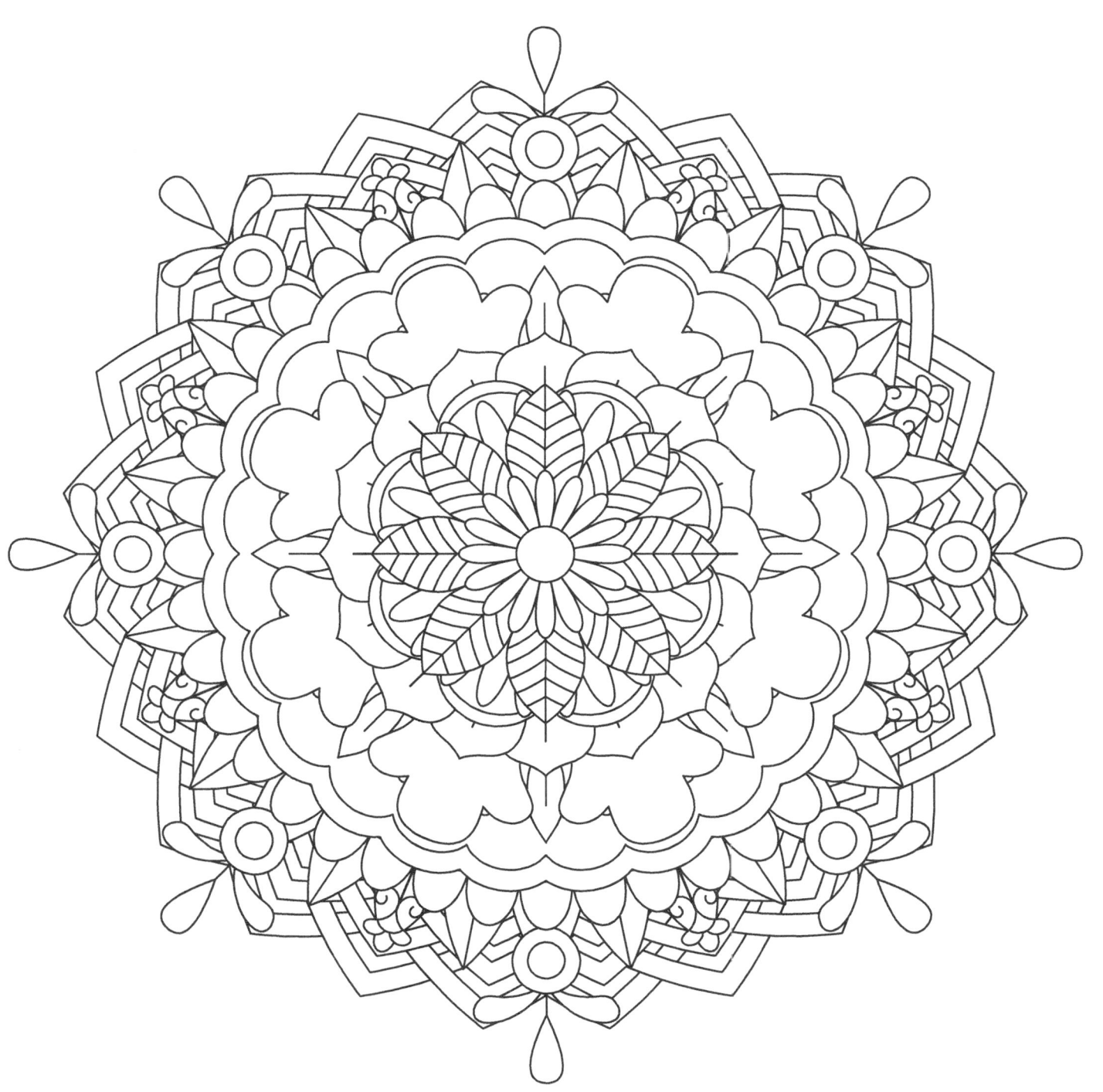

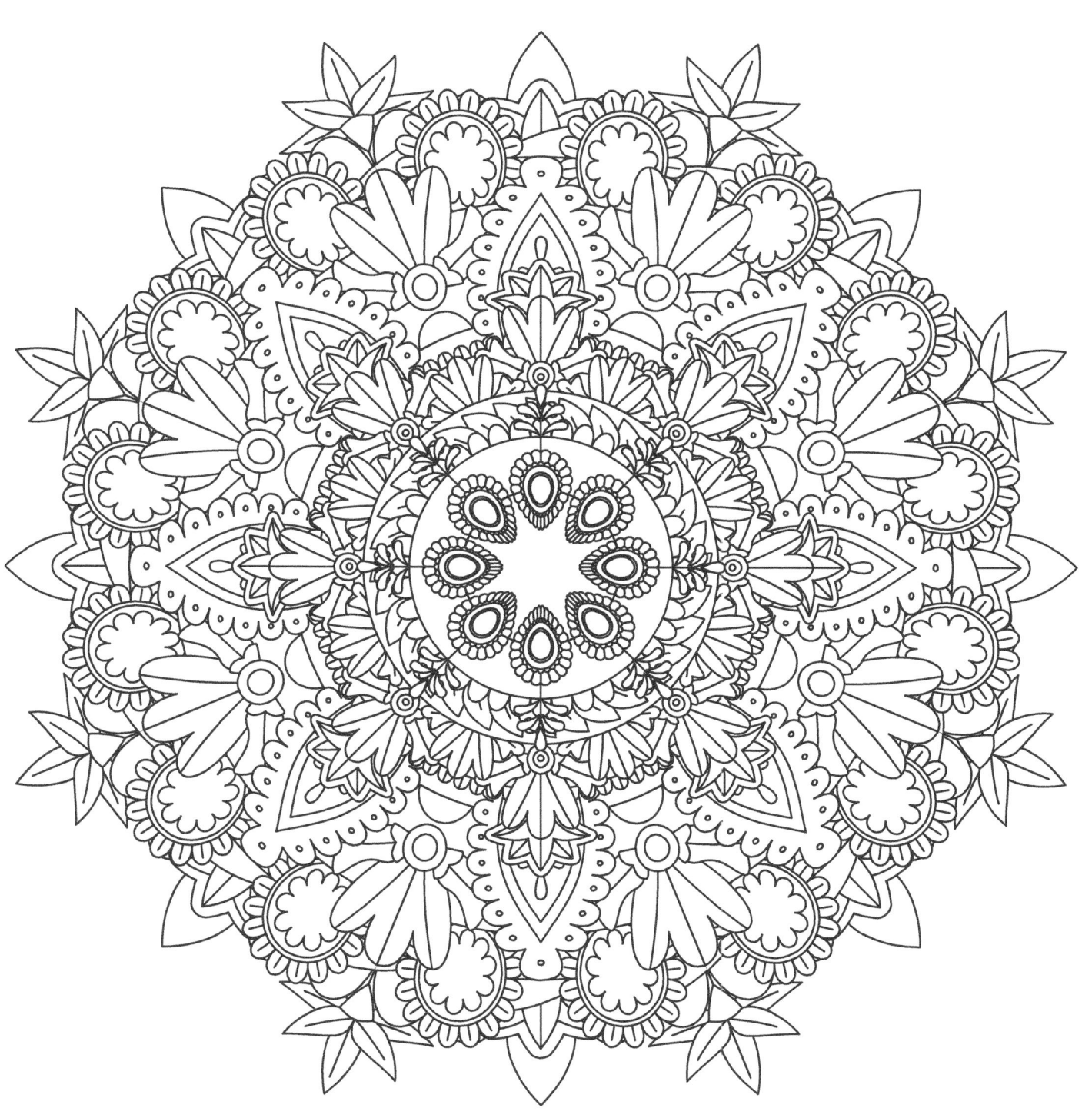

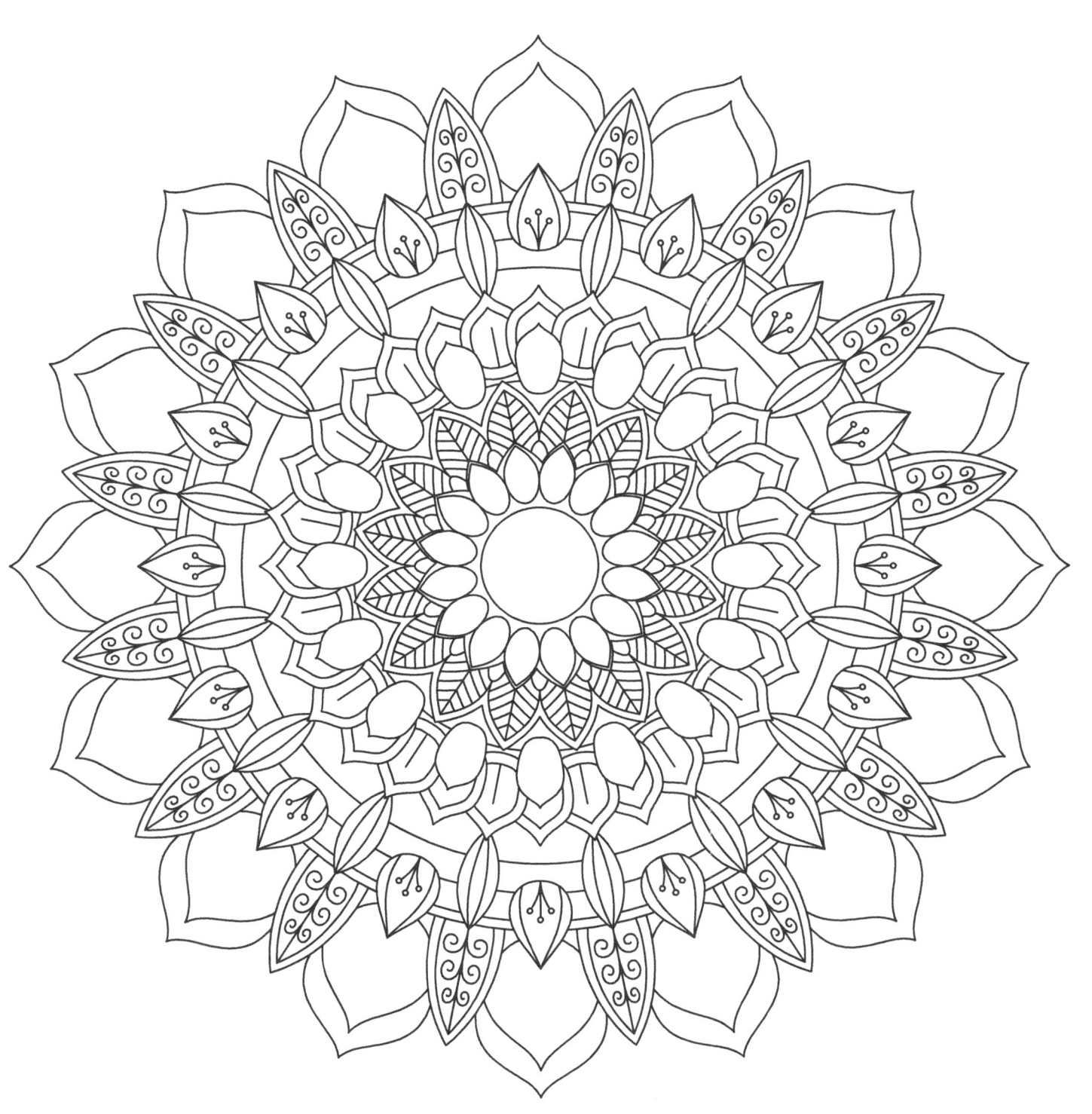

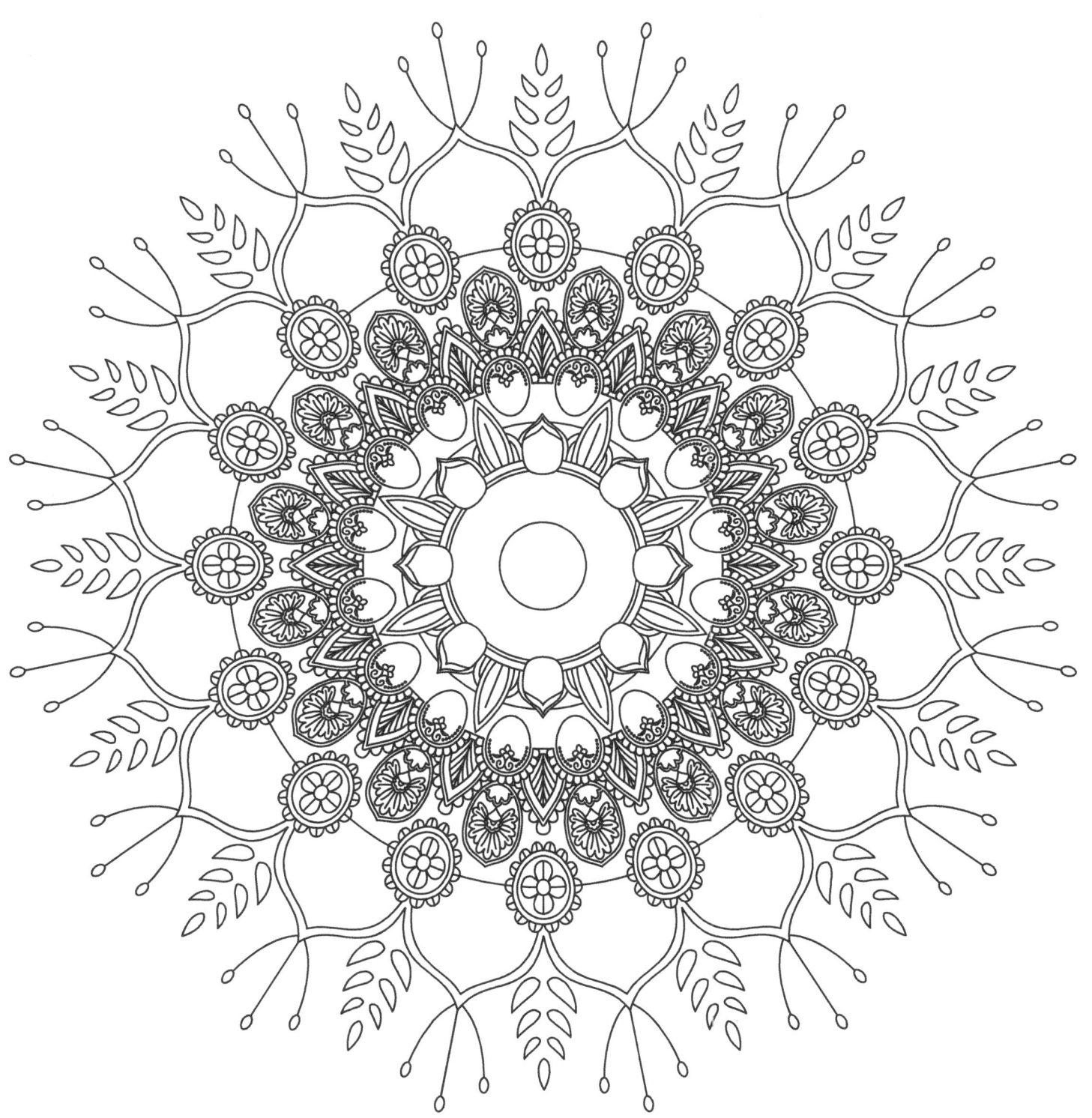

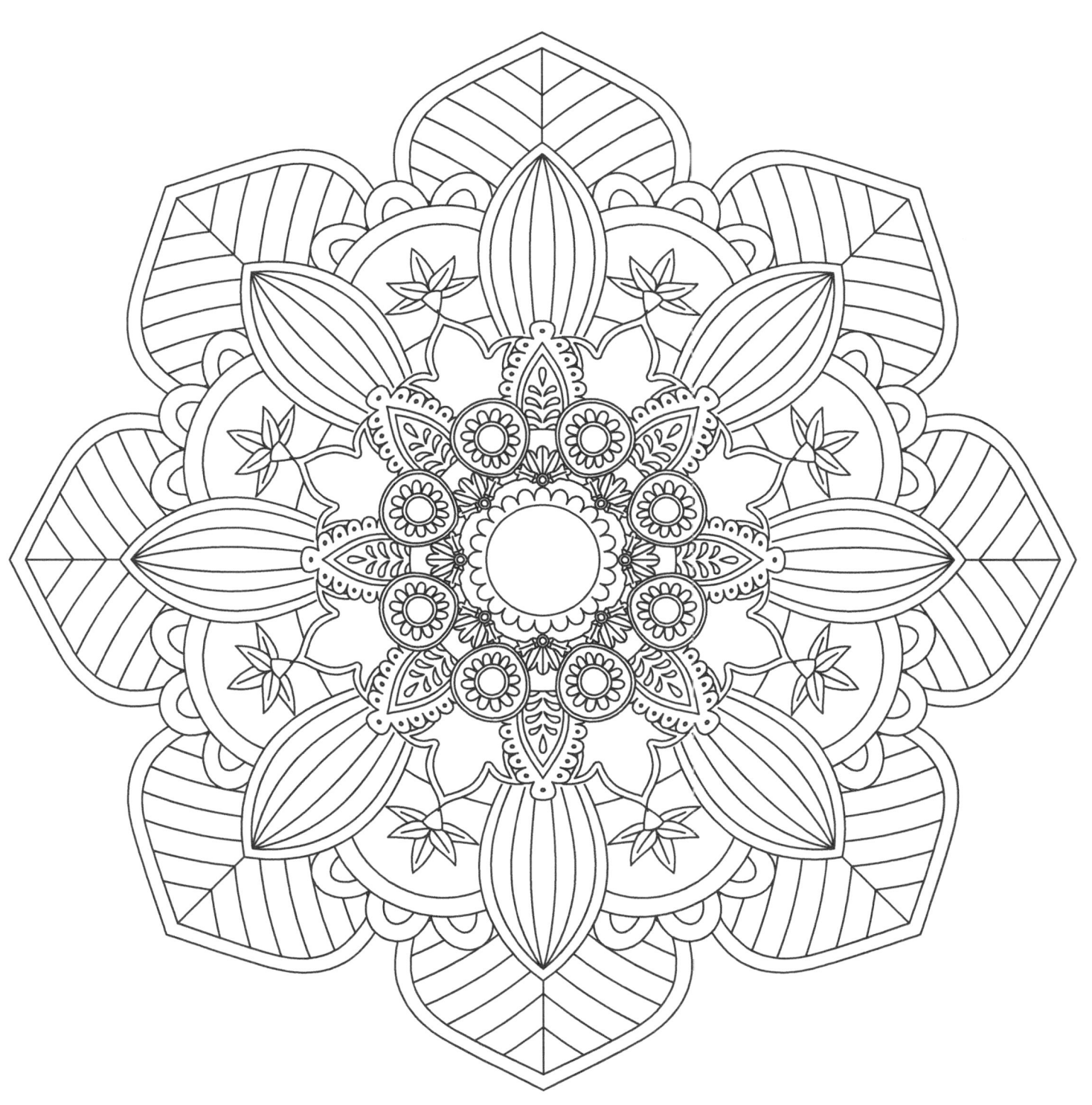

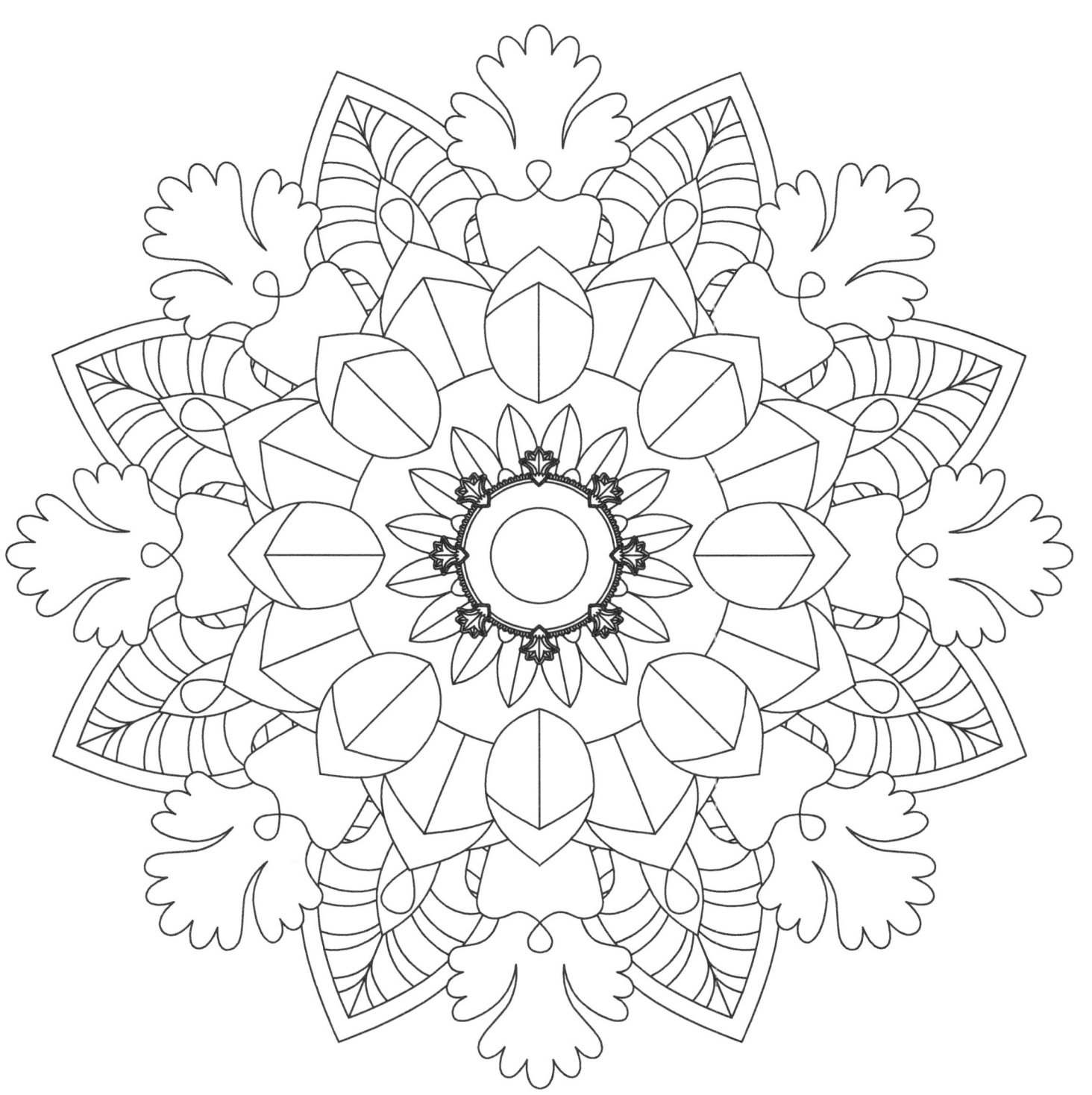

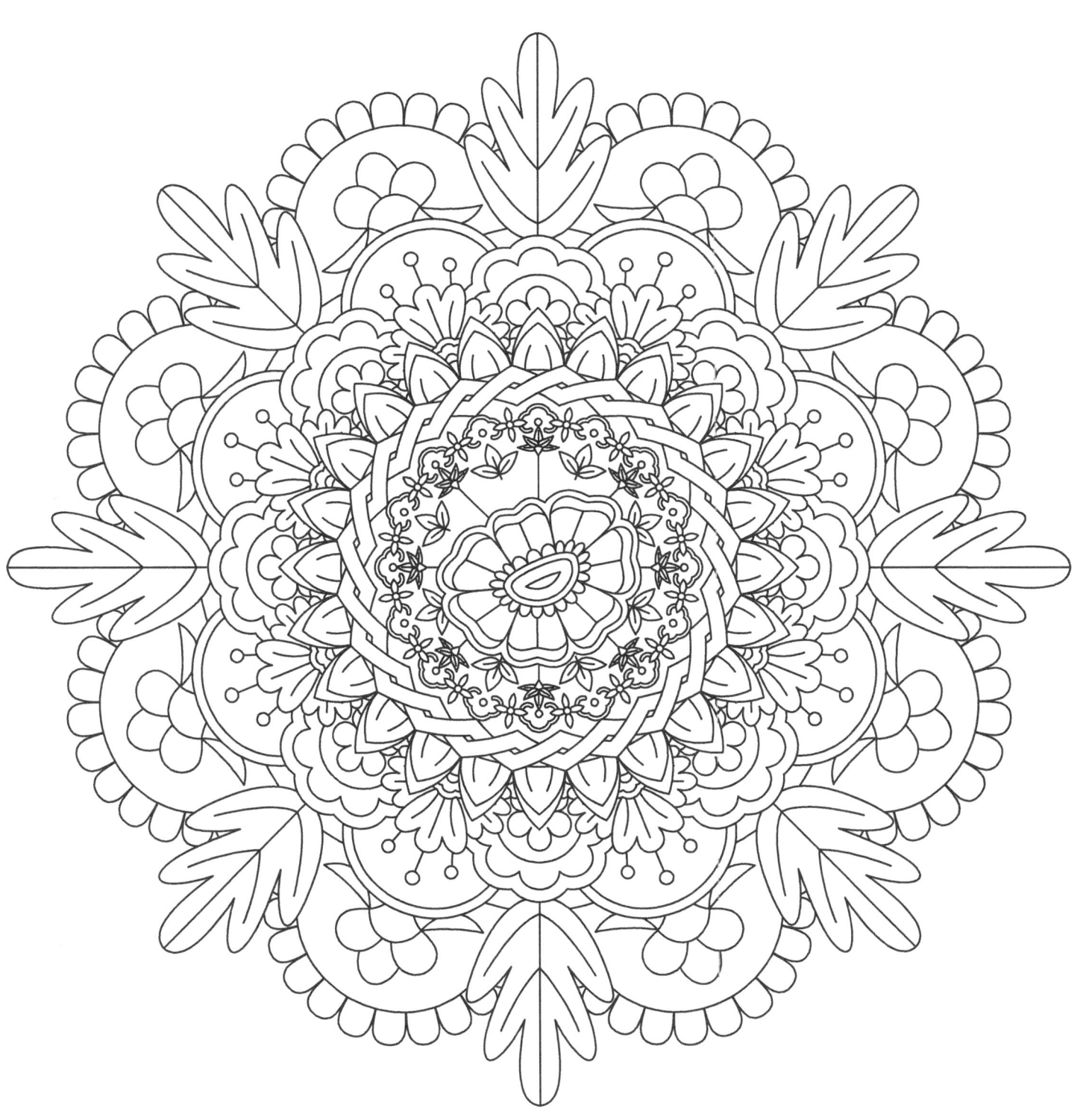

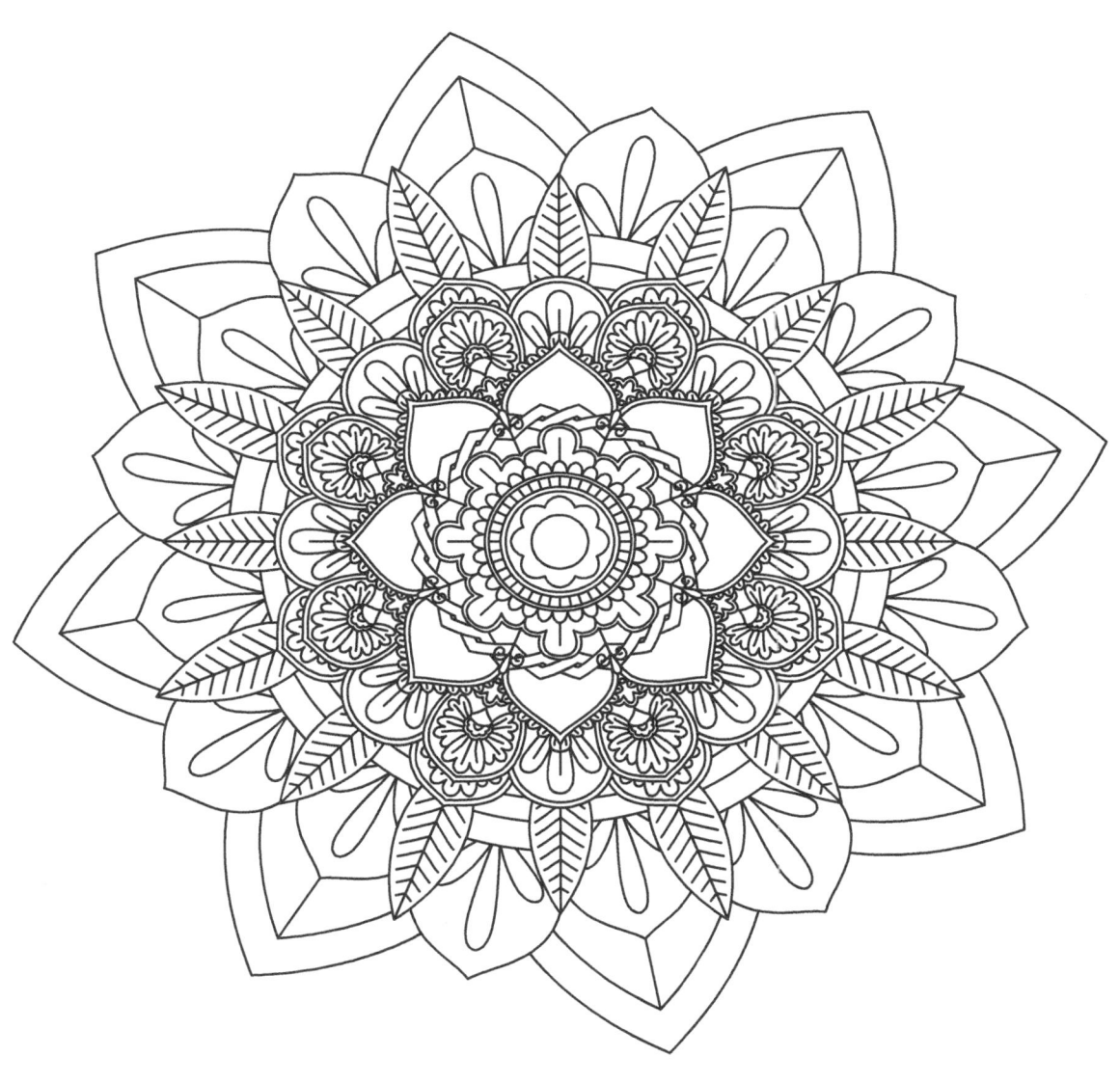

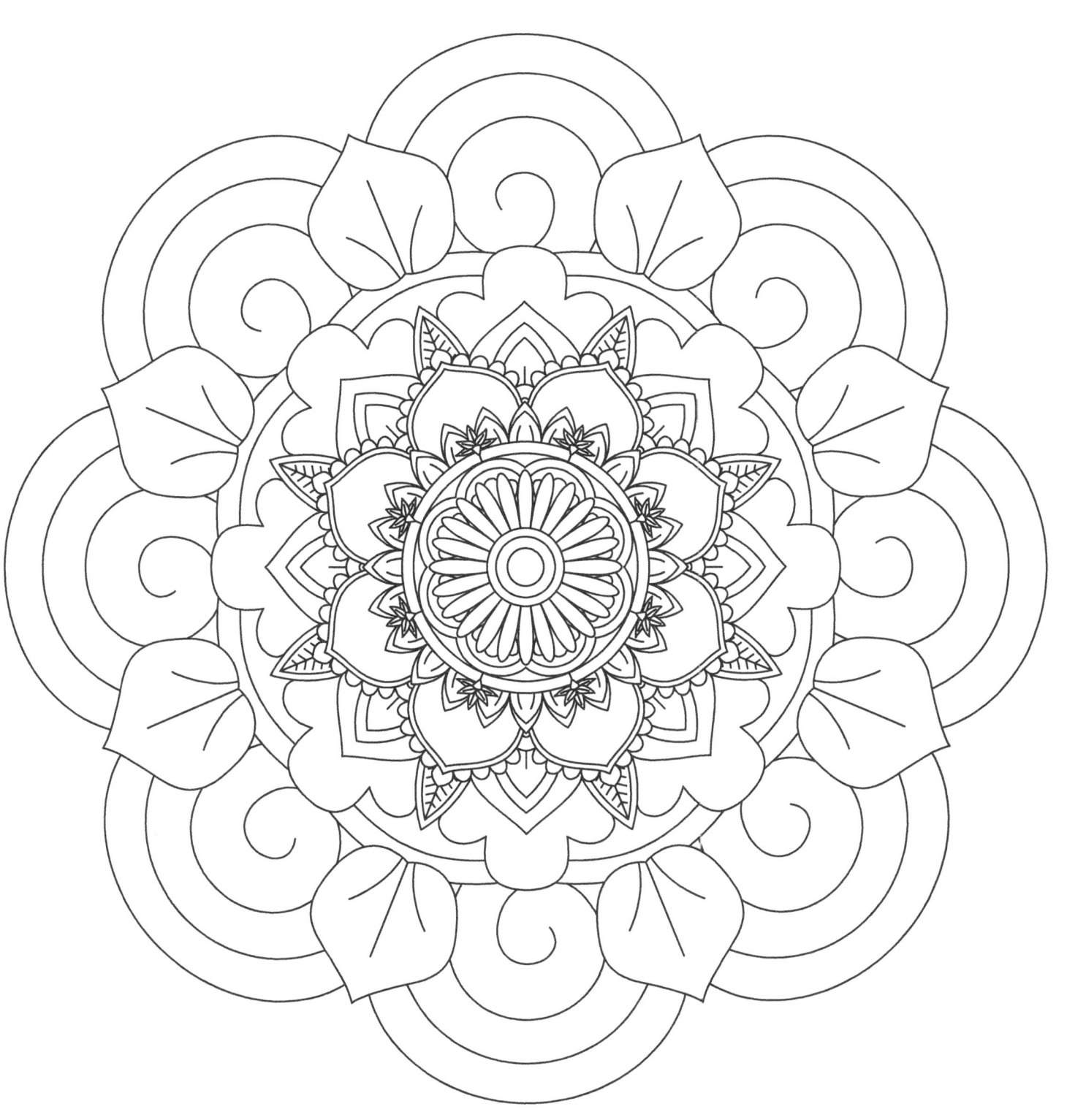

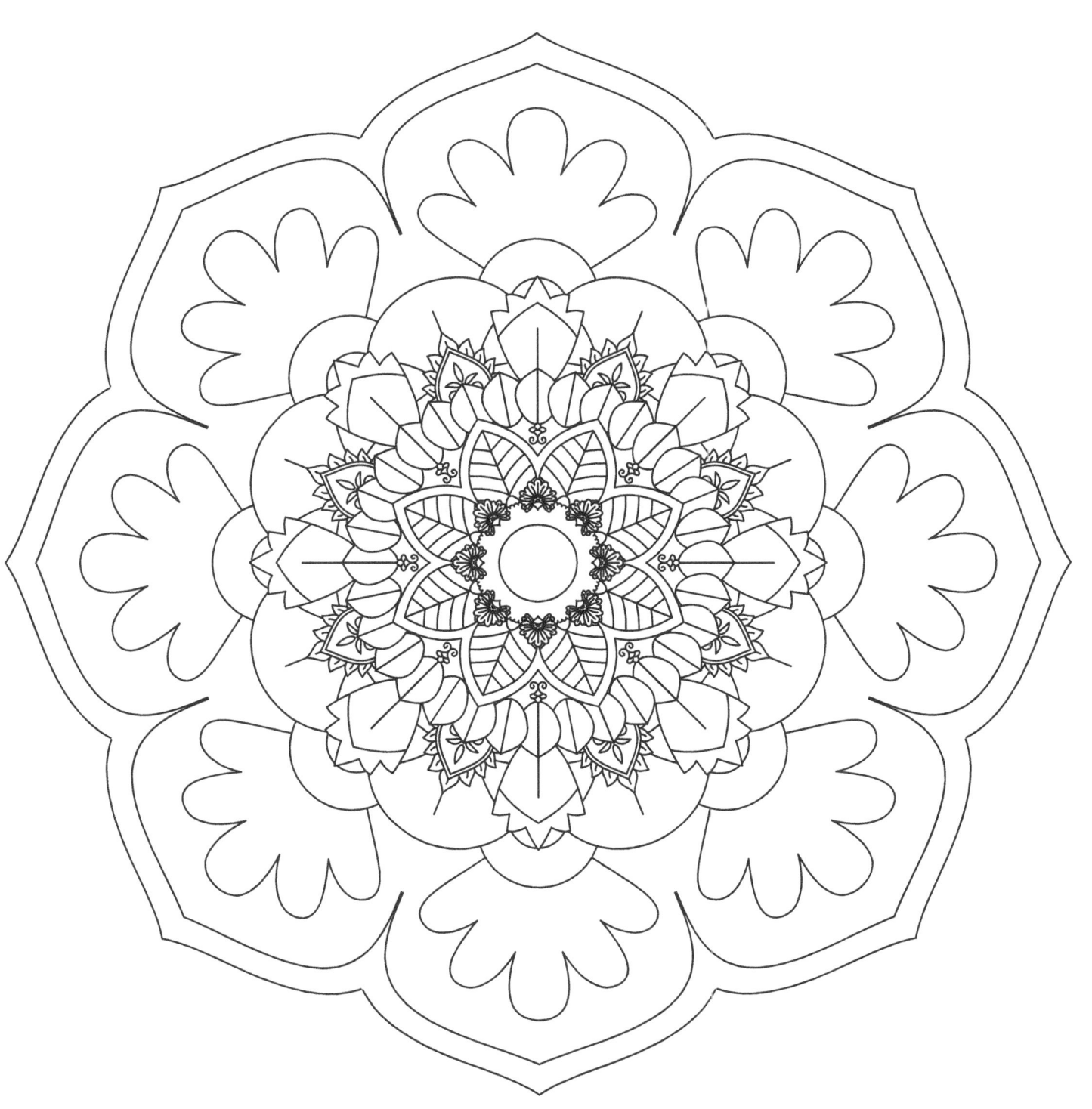

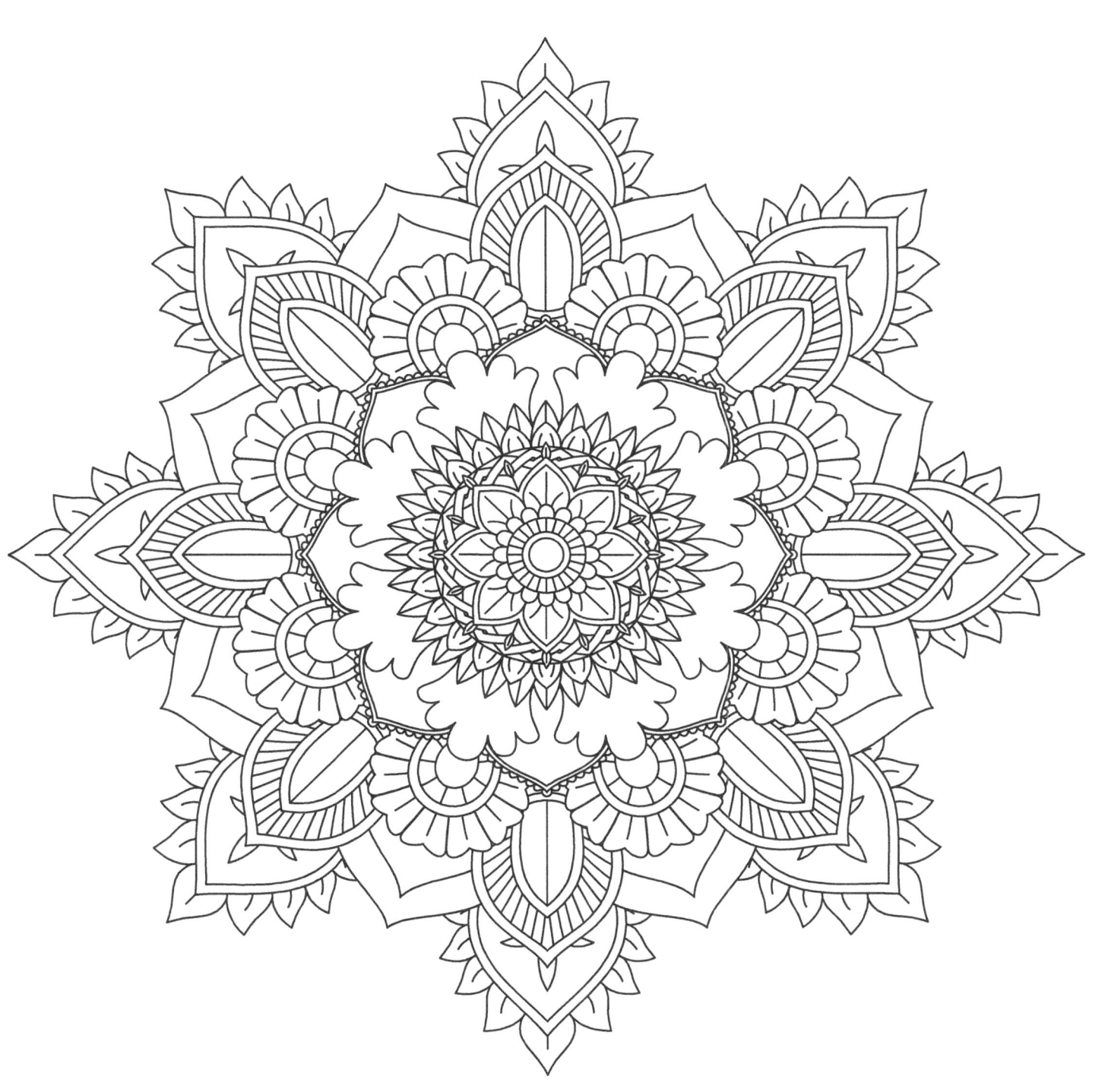

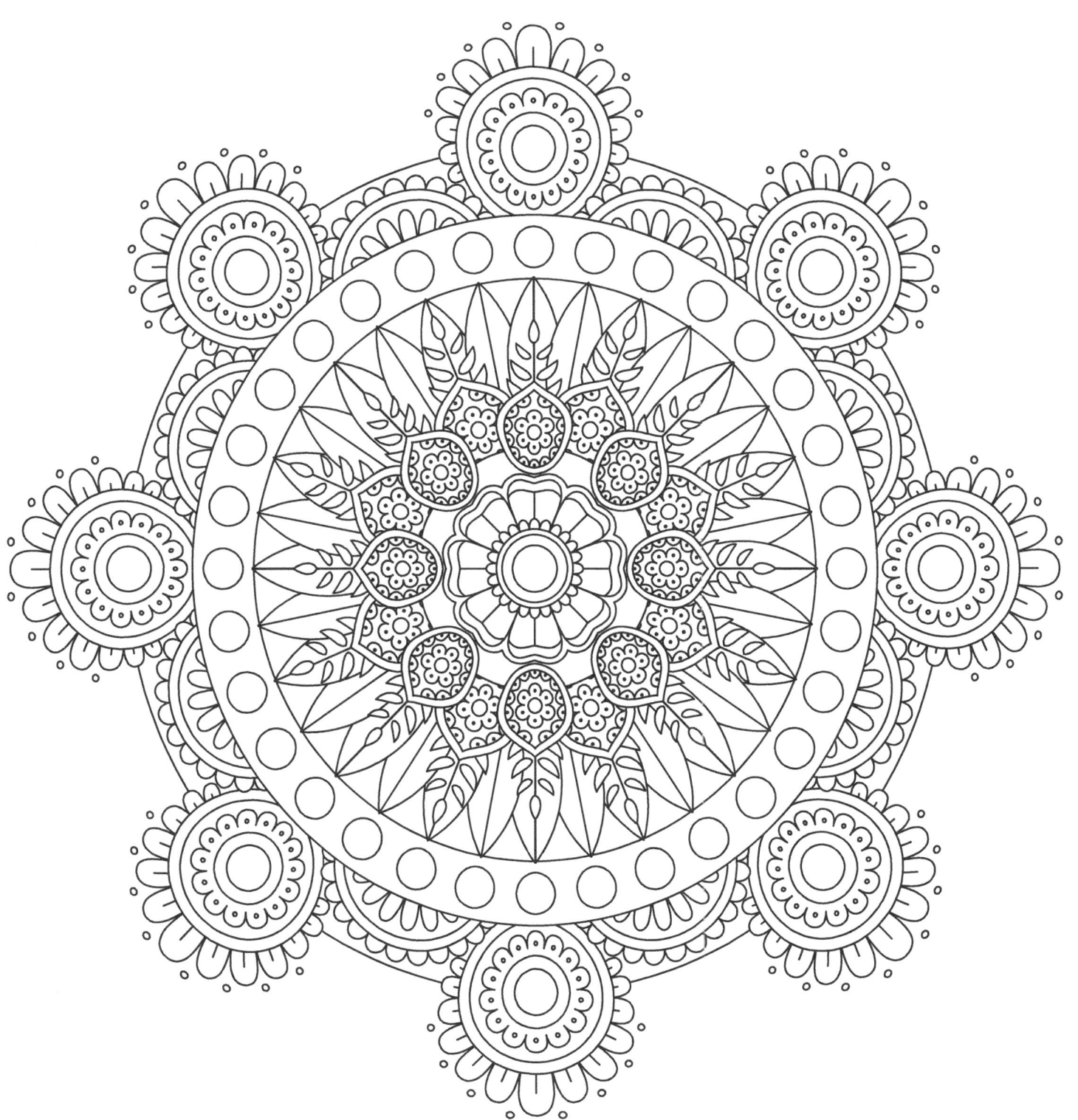

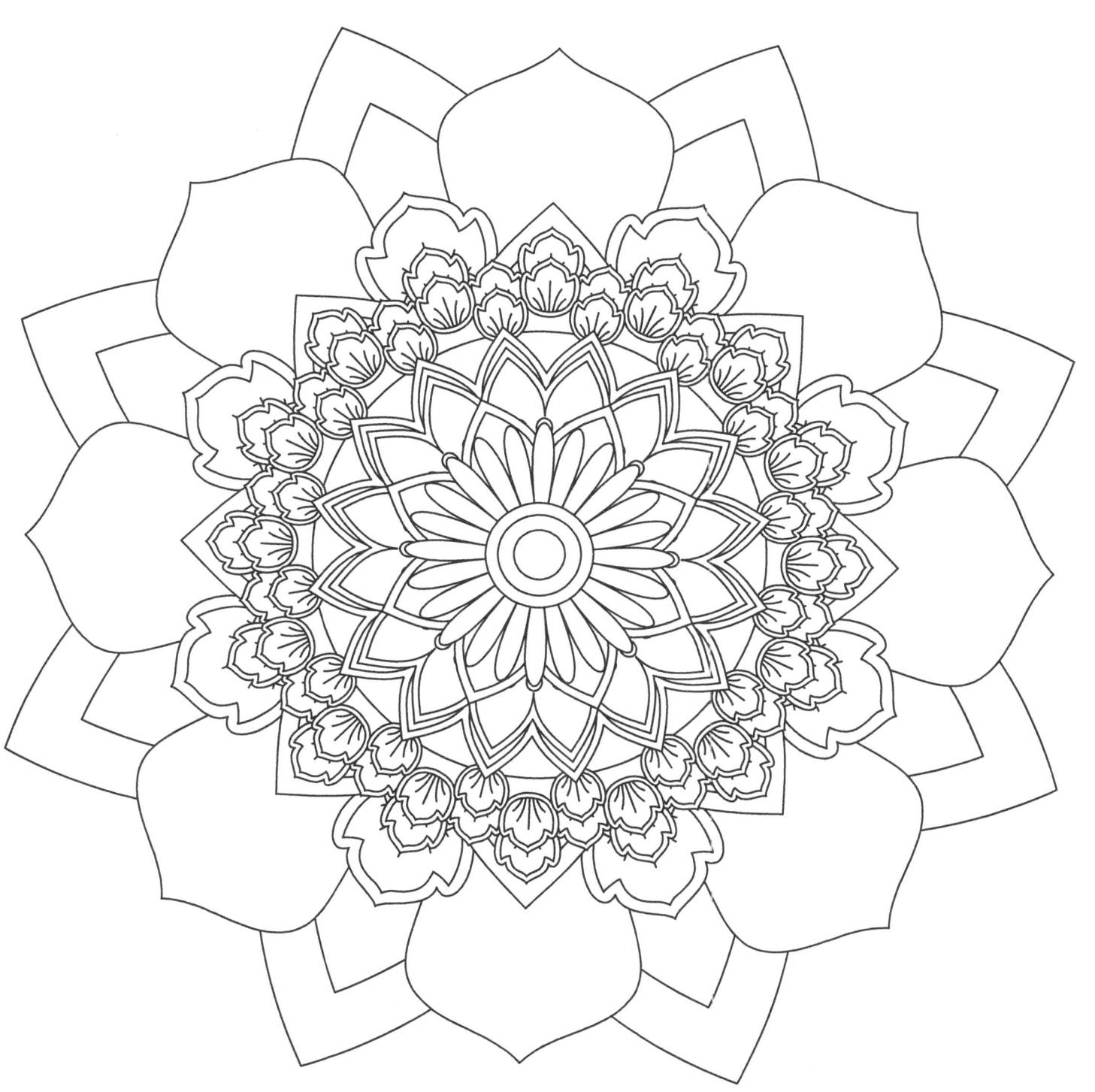

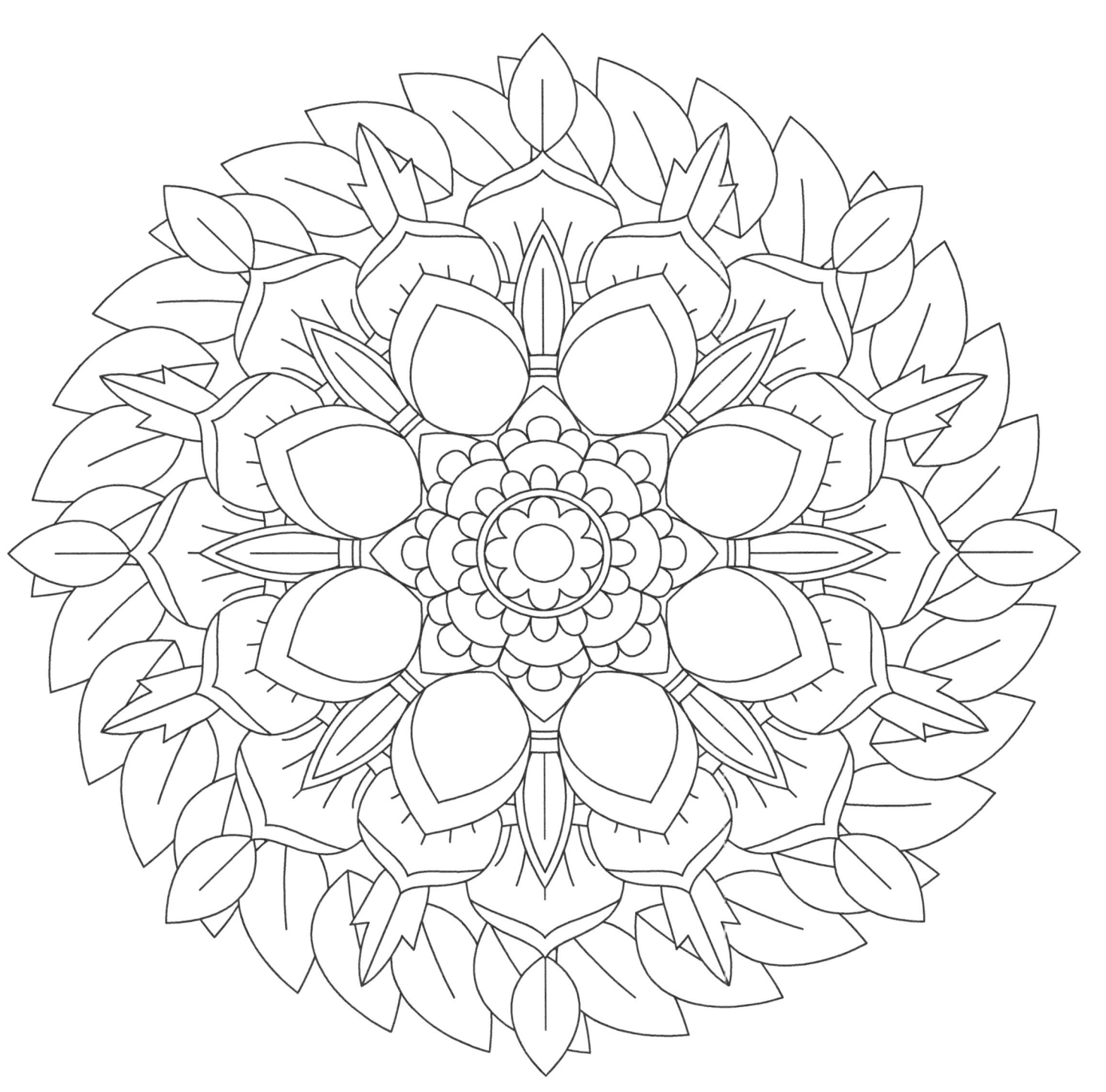

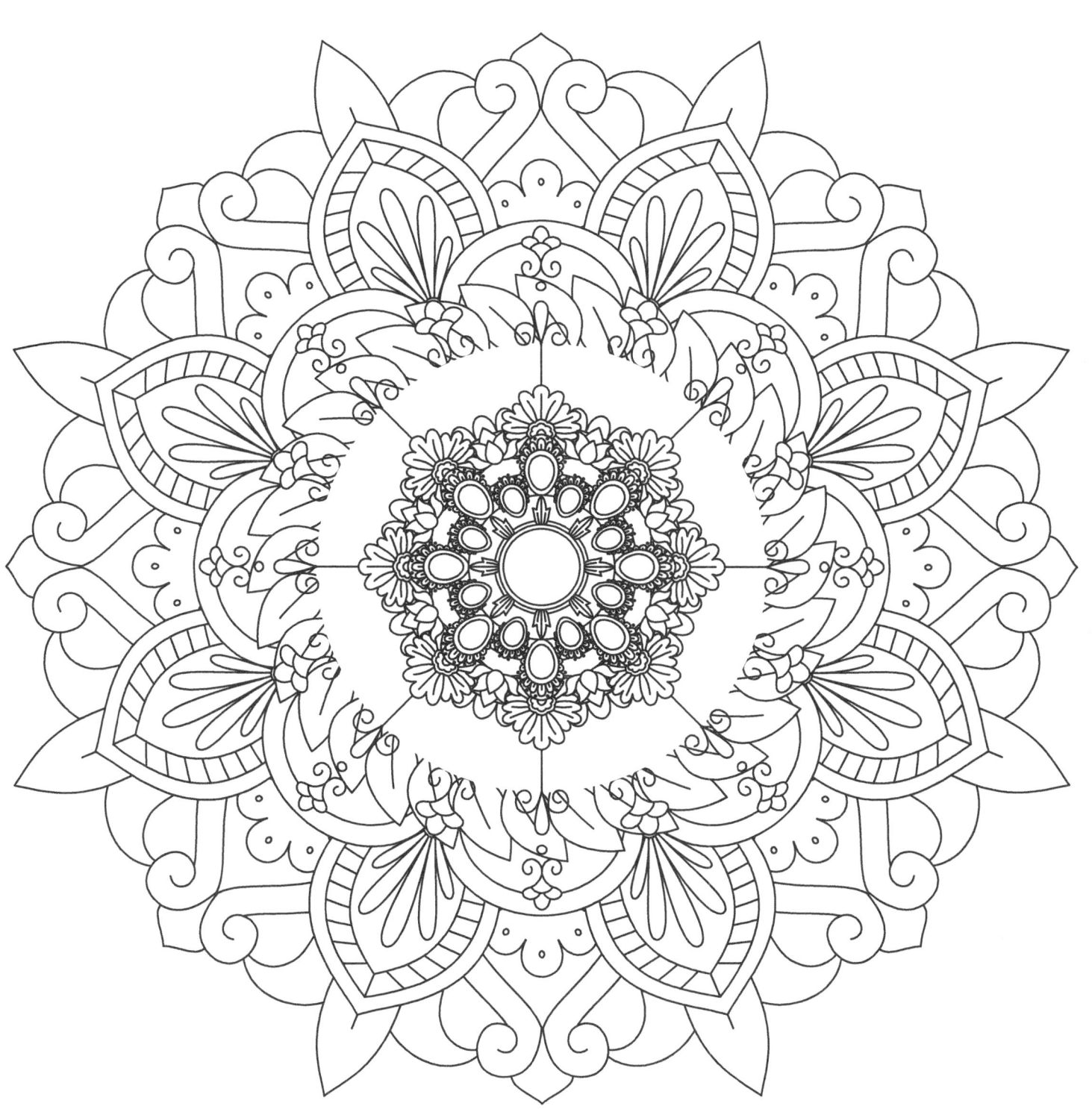

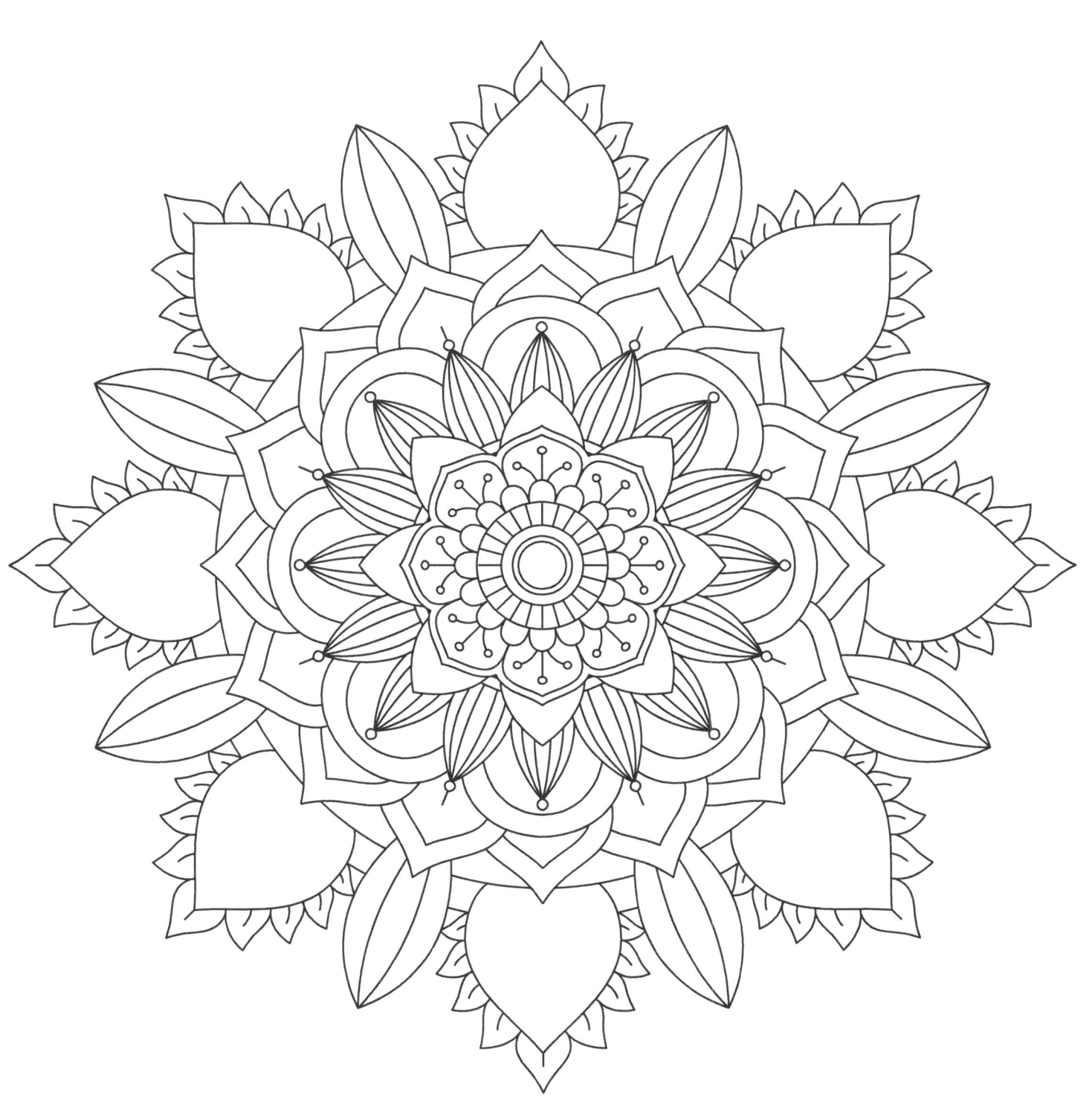

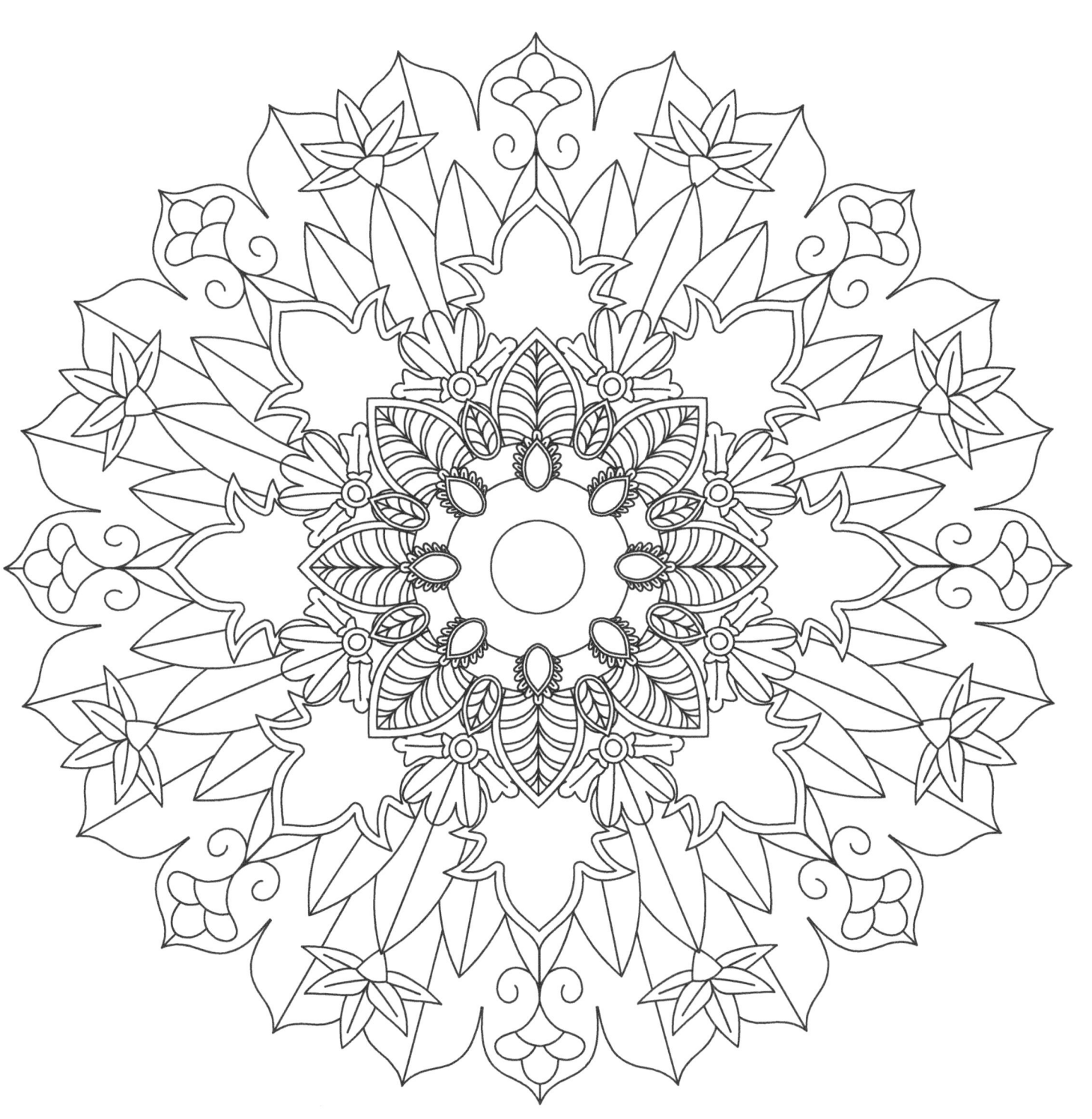

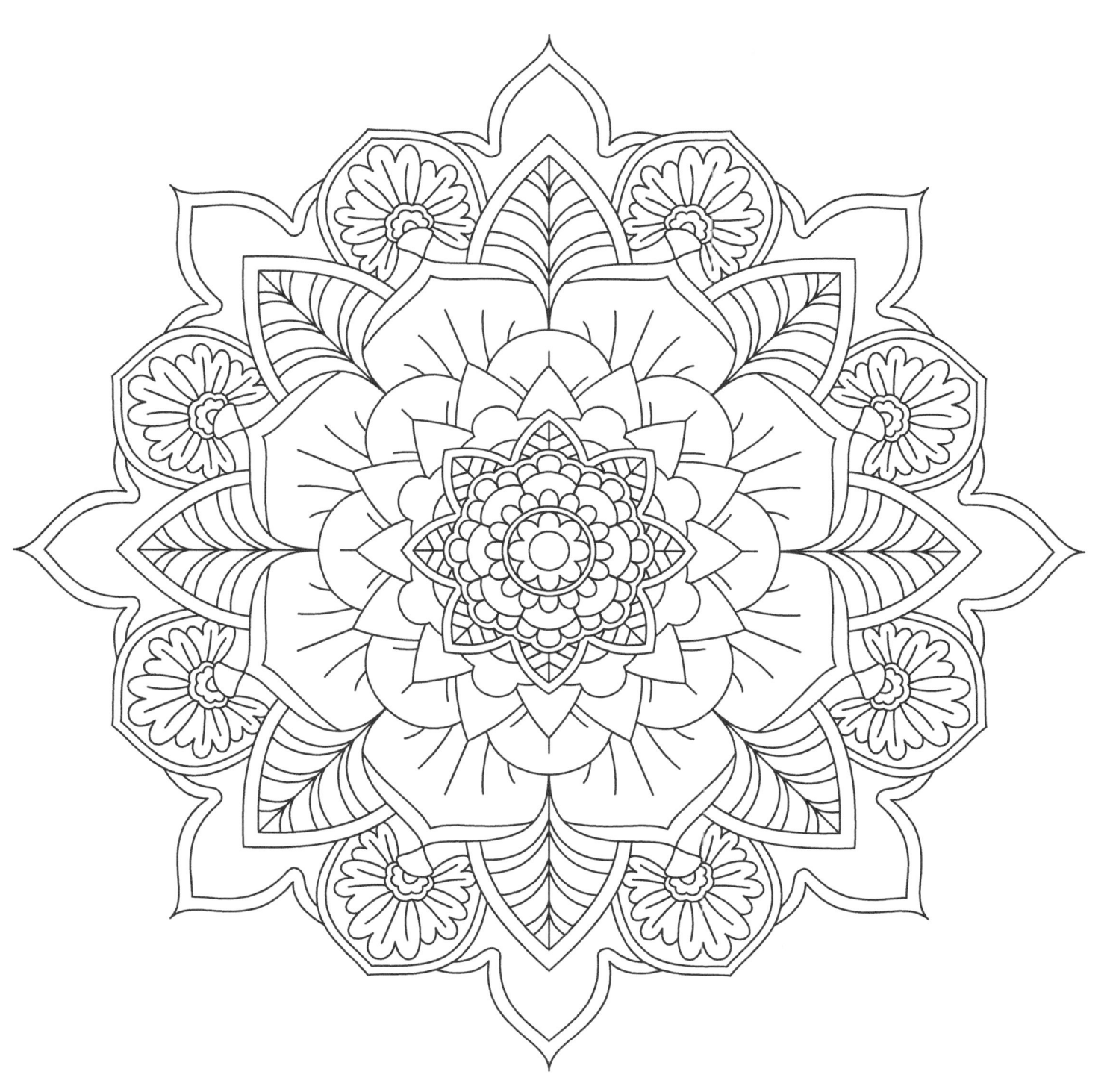

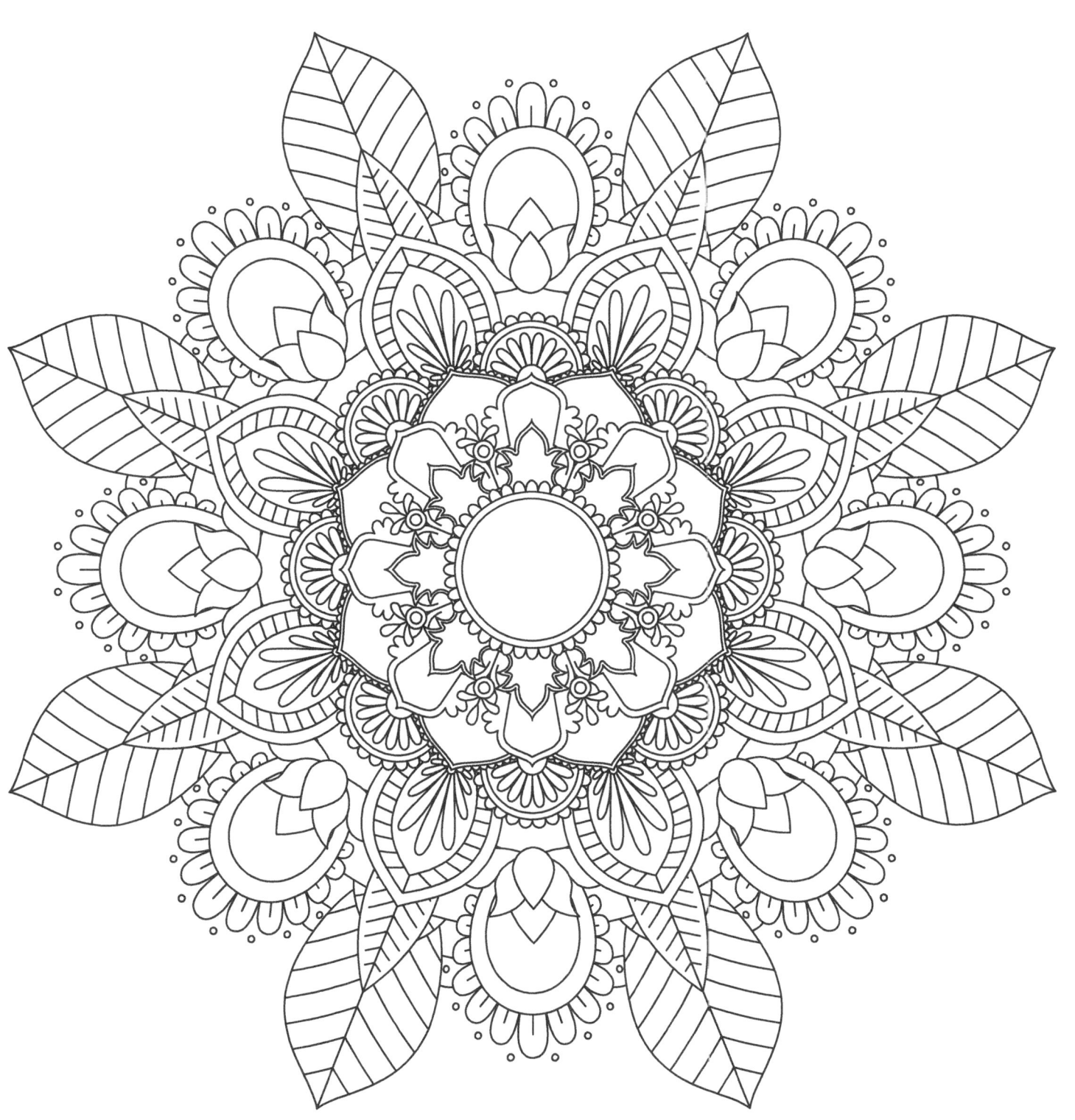

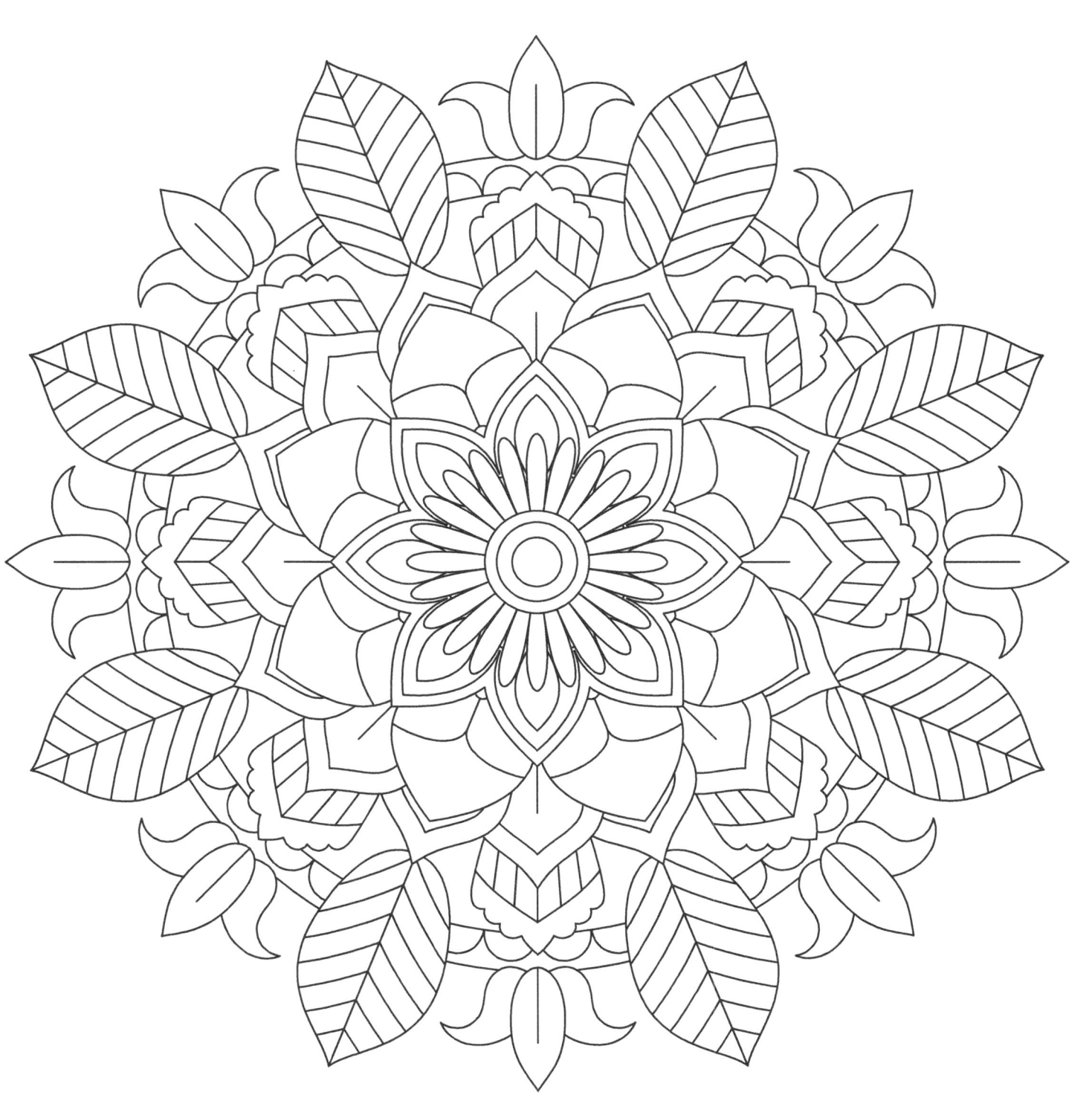

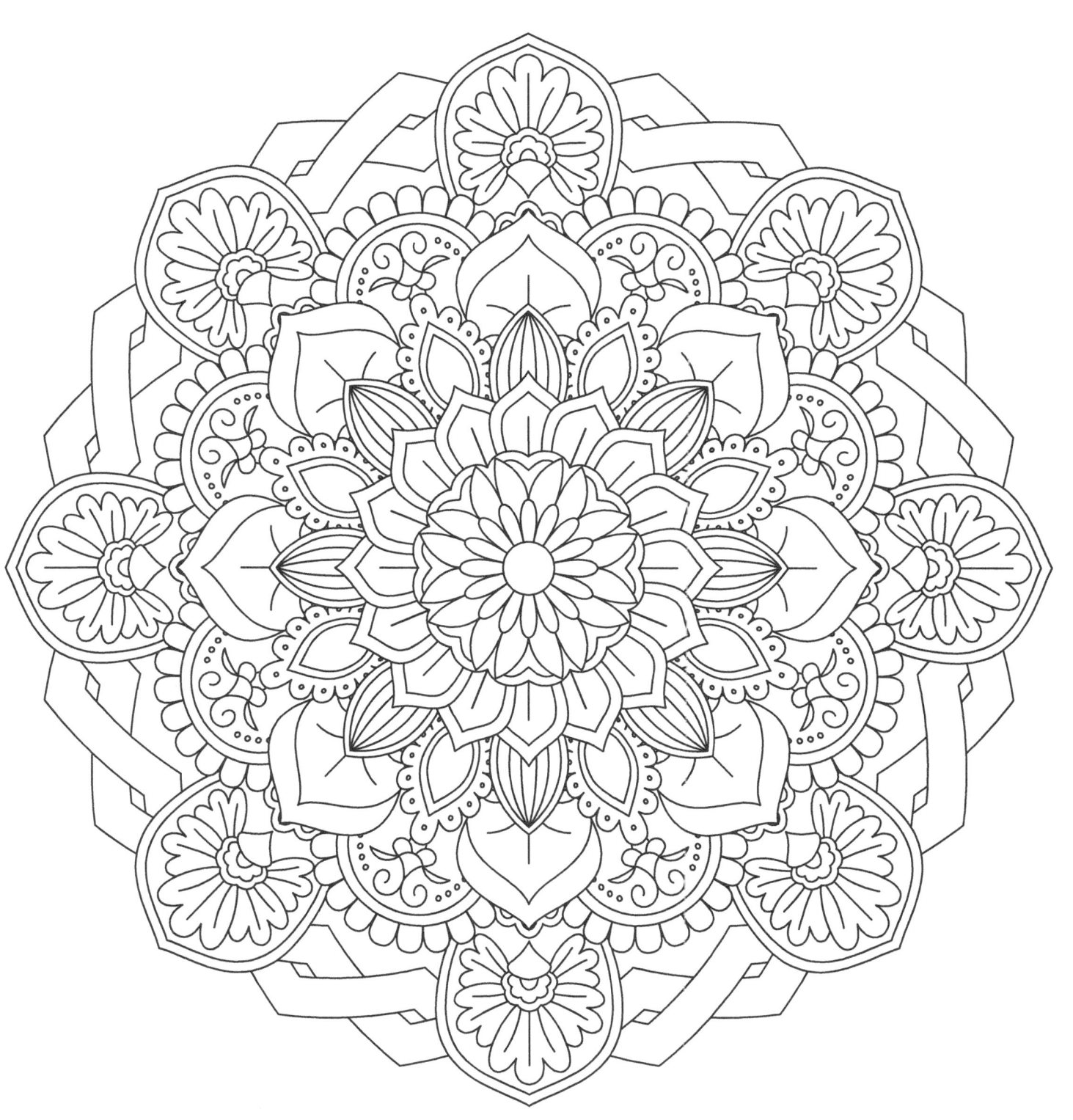

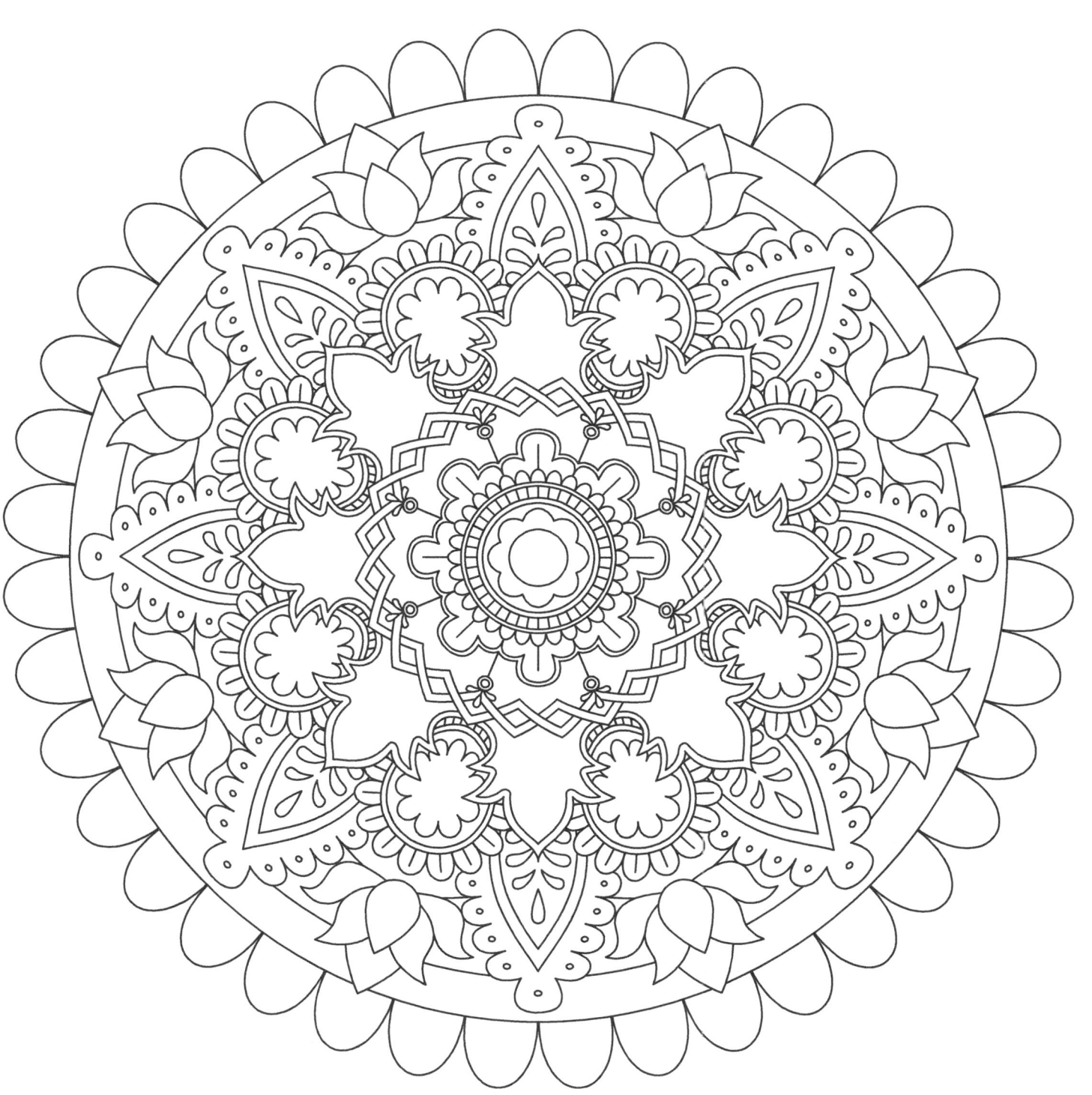

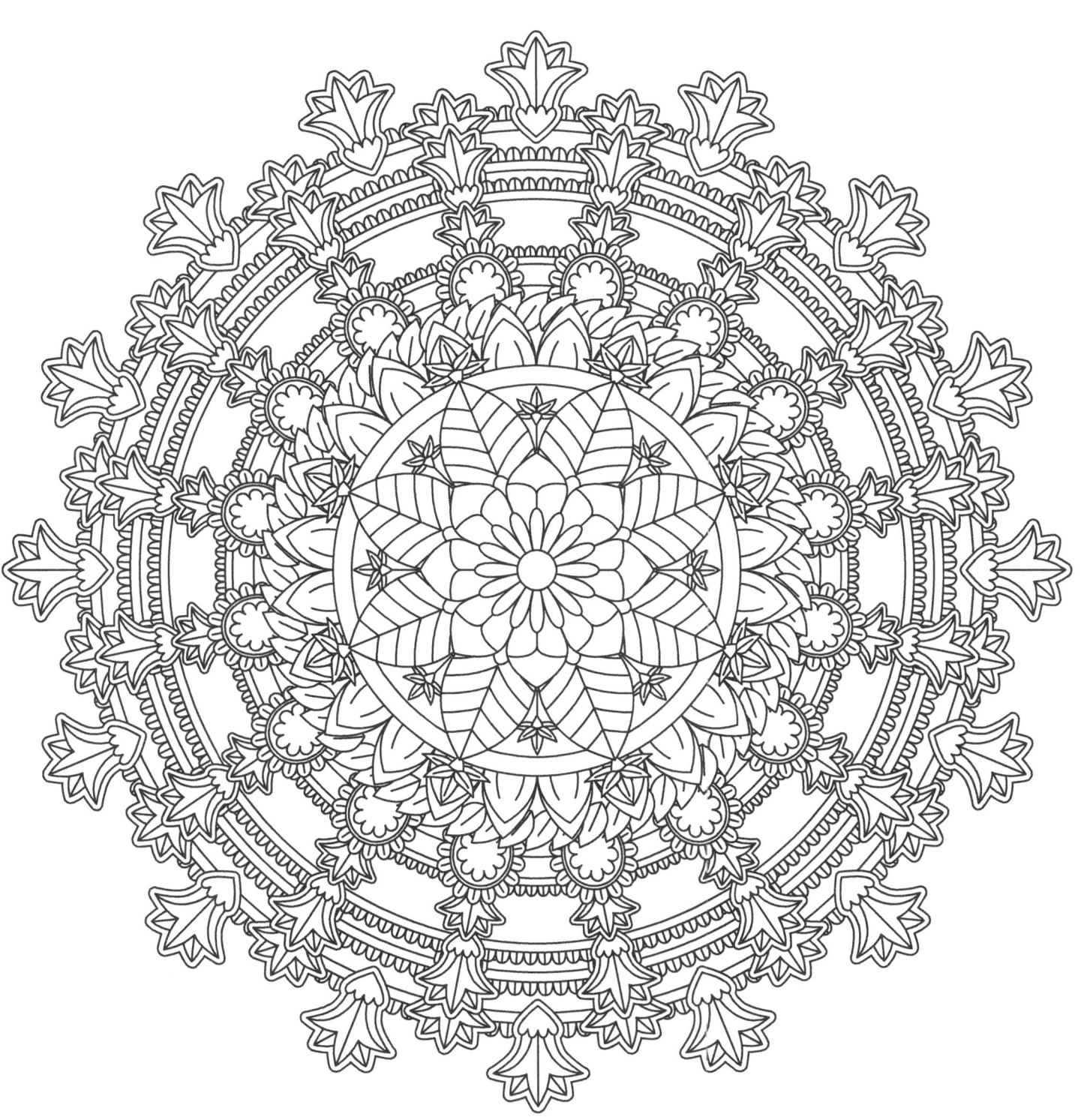

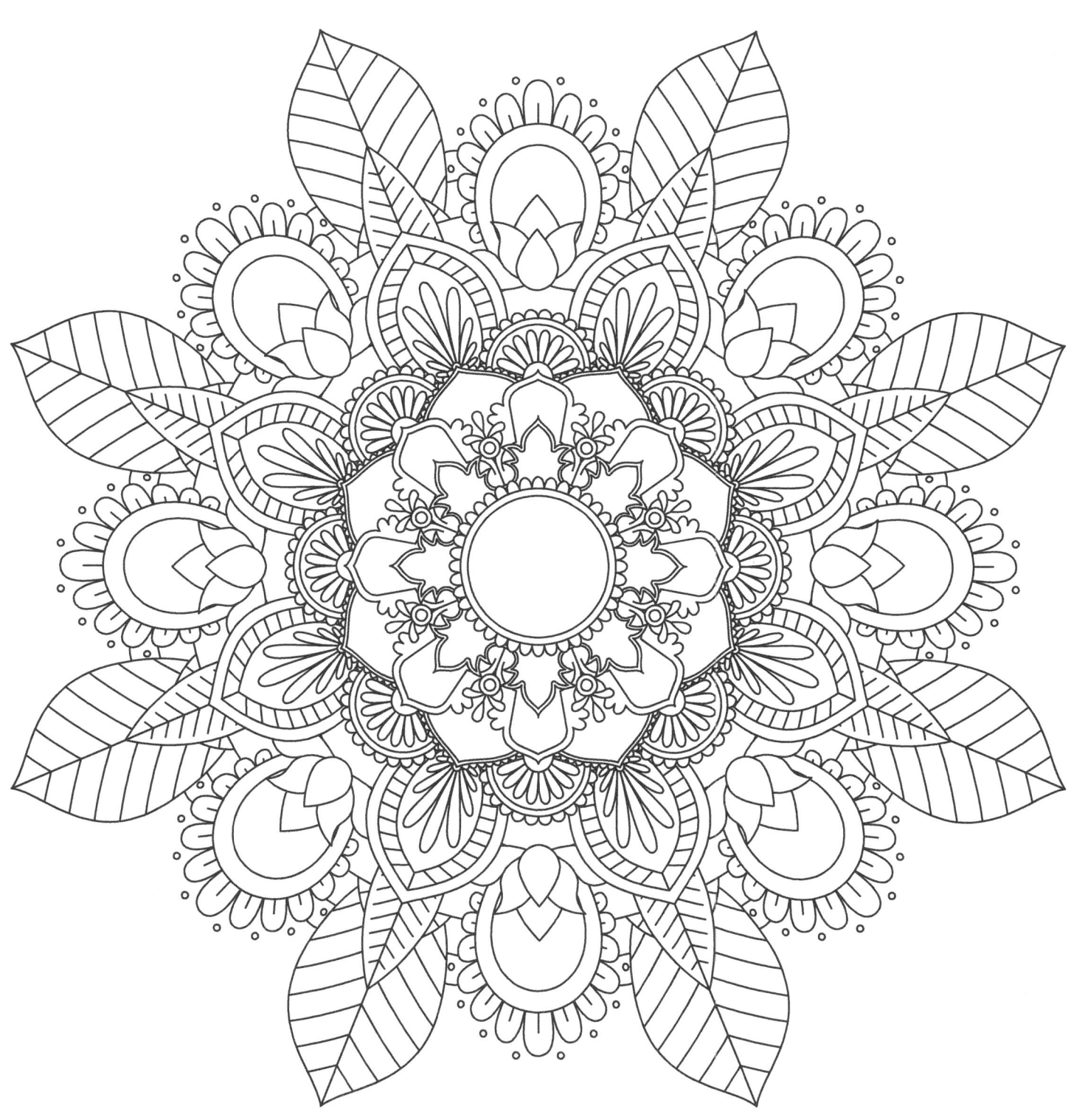

www.ingramcontent.com/pod-product-compliance
Lightning Source LLC
Chambersburg PA
CBHW080604220526
45466CB00010B/3245